SIR JOSEPH WILSON SWAN, F.R.S.

LOCAL INTEREST   £5.00

With Compliments
& Best Wishes

Austin McGuckin.
Dec 68

SIR JOSEPH WILSON SWAN, F.R.S.

AT THE AGE OF 80

SIR
JOSEPH WILSON SWAN
F.R.S.

INVENTOR AND SCIENTIST

BY

MARY E. SWAN AND KENNETH R. SWAN

ORIEL PRESS

First published by
Ernest Benn Limited, 1929
Reprinted with Preface and Appendix added, 1968

SBN(68UK) 85362 048 2
Library of Congress Catalogue Card Number 68-57094

Published by
Oriel Press Limited
at 27 Ridley Place, Newcastle upon Tyne, NE1 8LH, England
Printed by
Hindson & Andrew Reid Ltd., Newcastle upon Tyne

CONTENTS

CHAPTER X

PAGE

CHAPTER XI

CHAPTER XII

LIST OF ILLUSTRATIONS

PREFACE TO THIS EDITION

THE few hundred copies of this Memoir, printed in 1929 by Messrs. Ernest Benn Ltd. for distribution to relatives and friends of the Swan family, have long since been disposed of and the book is now out of print.

As it is, however, the sole complete record of my Father's life and work, and as there have been from time to time many enquiries as to where this Memoir could be obtained, particularly in view of the forthcoming dedication of a public memorial to Sir Joseph to be erected in Newcastle upon Tyne, it seemed to me to be desirable to issue a new edition of this Memoir. This Messrs. Hindson & Andrew Reid Ltd. in conjunction with Oriel Press Ltd have undertaken to do. The new edition is a facsimile reproduction of the original Memoir, with the addition (in an appendix) of a lecture delivered on 3rd February 1959 by Dr. Aldington, the distinguished scientist (and at that time Director of Associated Electrical Industries) to mark the eightieth anniversary of the invention and the first public demonstration of the Swan lamp, the first practical form of incandescent electric lamp with carbon filament, suitable for domestic lighting. This lecture was delivered in the lecture room of the Newcastle Literary and Philosophical Society, the identical room in which eighty years previously, namely on 3rd February 1879, my father delivered a lecture explaining his invention and showing the brilliant illumination which his lamps gave.

Kenneth R. Swan

Erratum—Page 122 penultimate line.   Sir Joseph, though one of its oldest members, did not become a President of the Pharmaceutical Society.   He delivered an address at the opening session of the Society's School of Pharmacy in 1903, normally a function of the President.

CHAPTER I

JOSEPH WILSON SWAN was born in the year 1828. During a long and laborious life he made many discoveries and inventions covering a wide range of scientific interest and industrial utility. Few of his inventive ideas proved unfruitful or failed to leave their mark upon the arts or manufactures to which they related. Some of them, notably his inventions in connection with photography and electric lighting, have formed the basis of important industries, and have resulted in widespread application and use. Amongst these are to be reckoned, for example, the *carbon process*, better known in this country as the " Autotype " process ; *bromide printing paper*, familiar to all photographers ; the *incandescent carbon filament electric lamp* ; the *cellular lead plate electrical storage battery*, and perhaps most important of all, *artificial cellulose thread*, the prototype of artificial silk. The products and derivatives of these inventions have become the familiar objects of everyday life, and are now accepted so completely as a matter of course that their origin and their author are alike in danger of being forgotten. That is natural enough. Nevertheless it is only right that, as we enjoy the conveniences of modern life and pride ourselves upon contemporary achievements of science, we should occasionally be reminded of those pioneers upon whose work this fabric of comfort, convenience, and æsthetic enjoyment has been built up. Joseph Swan was one of these pioneers ; and the object of this short biographical sketch is to recall and record, in the interests of history, the contribution which he made to the scientific progress of his time.

As the vista of years lengthens, and the past recedes into that dim haze which lies beyond the horizon of living memory, the perspective alters, and one is apt to under-estimate the magnitude of the advance that has been made in the appliances of everyday life.   Consider, for example, the amazing transformation that has taken place in public and domestic lighting, and contrast the present-day conveniences with those of a century ago.   Here is the picture of the conditions which prevailed when Joseph Swan first saw the light.   " The days of my youth," he writes in his old age, " extend backward to the dark ages, for I was born when the rush-light, the tallow-dip, or the solitary blaze of the hearth were common means of indoor lighting, and an infrequent glass bowl, raised 8 or 10 feet on a wooden post, and containing a cupful of evil-smelling train-oil with a crude cotton wick stuck in it, served to make darkness visible out of doors.   In the chambers of the great, the wax candle or, exceptionally, a multiplicity of them, relieved the gloom on state occasions, but as a rule the common people, wanting the inducement of indoor brightness such as we enjoy, went to bed soon after sunset.   For these were the days of the watchman with his lantern and rattle, who prudently warned off the prowling thief by a vociferous announcement of his coming, and the time of night, coupled with sundry details of wind and weather."   Passing on to note other conditions of those early times he continues : " These were the days of wooden ships, the stage coach, the 6d. newspaper, and the 1s. letter, the days of flint and steel, of the Brown Bess and the three decker, days not far removed from Waterloo and Trafalgar, when tales were still told to the children of the scare of Paul Jones and the dreaded French invasion, when half the people of Sunderland fled the town in deadly fear and lived in tents on Tunstal Hope.   ' *Bony* shall have you,' was still a potent threat to naughty children, and the Press Gang a recent memory."

Into this world, still full of memories of the great conflict and with the ferment of new ideas arising out of it, Joseph Wilson Swan was born on the Eve of All Hallows, in the year 1828, at Sunderland.

His father and mother, John and Isabella Swan, both belonged to families of Scotch descent which had settled in the county of Durham about the middle of the eighteenth century. They came of a sturdy stock engaged in pursuits which enabled them to live in a fair degree of comfort and to bring up healthy children in the bracing air of the north-east coast. Some of their forbears were yeoman farmers, some seafaring folk, whilst others were engaged in trade and manufacture more or less connected with shipping.

The situation of Sunderland and the adjoining town of Bishop Wearmouth naturally shaped the lives of many of its inhabitants and gave them a sea-bent; for the chief concern and occupation of both towns came by way of the sea, from the business of building, provisioning and manning ships, from the handling of their cargoes, and from all the world-wide interests of their voyages and traffickings.

It was the misfortune of John Swan (Joseph's father) that he was withheld from following his natural inclination for a seafaring life. His father, a merchant captain owning his own ship, had died at sea, and John's mother could not overcome her fear of it for her only son. So John Swan had to content himself with a comfortable business ashore, making and selling ships' anchors and chains and such-like ironmongery.

All his life his thoughts turned to the sea, and, being of an inventive frame of mind, he devised various nautical appliances: an anchor with movable flukes, a life-saving raft and launching apparatus, and a system of fog-signalling for preventing collisions at sea.

From time to time John Swan was able to gratify his taste for seafaring. He made several voyages as supercargo on merchant ships belonging to different members of the family, and on one occasion he acted as captain.

Even after he was seventy years old he embarked upon a sea-venture. Together with Captain Wiggins (of Kara Sea fame) he chartered a ship and sailed to Iceland to bring back a cargo of sheep. The voyage was disastrous. It was undertaken too late in the year, and too large a cargo of sheep was taken on board, with the consequence that it had to be jettisoned in a terrific storm which was encountered on the homeward voyage.

To the end of his life he was making experimental models of his devices ; a gentle, sturdy old man, a keen politician and full of stories of the past.

Though fitted by aptitude and inclination for a sea-faring life, John Swan was but poorly endowed with those qualities which make for success in business. He was easy-going and generous to a fault—always ready to help others to his own detriment. He was fond of new ideas and was constantly engaging in fresh ventures—losing money on each enterprise.

" But e'en his failings leaned to virtue's side," and in spite of ill-success in business, which deprived his children of an easy start in life, they inherited from him many fine qualities—generosity and gentleness, integrity and enter-prise, good brains and sound constitutions ; while the hardships of their growing years proved a stimulus to greater effort and heightened their appreciation of such advantages as they had.

In 1820, at the age of twenty-five, John Swan had married Isabella, daughter of George Cameron (a member of one of the septs of the Cameron clan), whose immediate forbears had settled in the village of Esh, Co. Durham.

George Cameron was a stone mason and master builder who had made a good position for himself early in life.

One of his buildings, the old Exchange (now used as a Seamen's Institute), still stands in the High Street at Sunderland as a witness of his work.

He was killed by the fall of a wall blown down in a great storm of the year 1814.[1]

---

[1] The event is thus recorded in Richardson's *Table Book*, vol. iii., p. 146: " A great hurricane commenced about sunrise and continued through the

The first home of John and Isabella Swan was in the Low Street at Sunderland, where he carried on his business. The back of the house overlooked the Wear, and the young wife used to be harrowed with the sounds of the cruel floggings of seamen on the men o' war in the river. But after the birth of a daughter, Elizabeth, happier surroundings were found, and a remove was made to Pallion Hall, a large house, with a garden sloping down to the Wear, about two miles up the river from Sunderland. Here two sons were born, John and Joseph, and this was the dearly remembered home of their childhood.

Sir Joseph Swan has left a graphic picture of the surroundings of this early home and of the impression they left upon his youthful mind. " There was a fine view of the river from the end windows of our house which looked across from a considerable height, enabling me to see the shipbuilding going on on the opposite side of the river, and ships and boats coming and going up and down. Among the things I remember at Pallion are the building of ships and ship launches, and now and then a little tug steamer.

"'Steamboats' were then quite new things. Steam power had not then bridged the Atlantic. It was still a question whether it could be done.

" The ships were then, of course, all built of wood— the heterodox idea of a ship of iron being capable of floating had not entered the public mind, let alone the possibility of its sailing, and the ships were all sailing ships then. I recall how beautiful they looked in every aspect, whether with sails full spread or in wintry bareness.

" And how beautiful the river was in all its sights and sounds ! Always beautiful ! The banks were very high, mountainous they seemed to my inexperienced eyes—

whole day, which did great damage in Newcastle and the neighbourhood. At Sunderland the gale blew with indescribable fury. About one o'clock, a garden wall on the east side of Nile Street, Bishop Wearmouth, was blown down, and Mr. George Cameron, a very respectable master mason of Sunderland, who was passing at the time, was so severely wounded in the head that he only survived three hours."

green where nature had been allowed to retain her pre-
dominance, but in places grey rock protruded and, bordering the ragged quay, there were strewn pell-mell heaps
of sheds and loose timber in picturesque confusion.   That
was across the river, but up or down it was the same feast
of beauty for seeing eyes.   Away from the riverside was
pure country with fields and farms.   I remember, with
a haunting fear, a great limestone-quarry with its alpine
precipices, as they seemed to me, that often troubled my
dreams in phantom forms inexpressibly horrid.   Then
there was the great range of lime kilns that bordered the
near side of the river bank and used up the produce of
the quarry.   There were also glass works near-by which I
was taken to see.   Lime-burning and glass bottle-making
were, therefore, the first manufacturing processes I had
the opportunity of seeing."

With all this stimulating activity around them the
children of the family developed quickly in intelligence.
Joseph in particular was interested in watching how things
were made and done.

The family life was of the happiest.   The cheerful and
loving dispositions of the parents were inherited by their
children.   An adaptation which they made of a Wesleyan
hymn, and which they were fond of singing, shows something of the joyousness of their young life.

> " And then we'll shout and shine and sing,
>   And make the Pallion arches ring
>   When all the Swans come home."

This mutual affection and happy intercourse endured
between the brothers and sisters all their lives, through
all the changes of fate and fortune.

Changes of fortune began early, and the pleasant years
at Pallion were few.   The working of the limestone
quarry situated on the Pallion property proved, like so
many of John Swan's ventures, unsuccessful, and it
became necessary to remove his family from there to a
smaller house at Olive Street, Sunderland.   Though

everything was on a reduced scale, except the family, which now consisted of four boys and four girls [1]—a fair degree of comfort was maintained, and the elder children were sent to the best schools the neighbourhood afforded.

Some reminiscences written by Sir Joseph Swan in his old age give a vivid picture of his early days.

"The patron of my early boyhood was an old captain —a great-uncle, my grandmother's brother, Commander John Kirtley, R.N., who had fought with distinction at sea under Nelson. In his delightful company I spent the happiest of these far-back years, and his constant care it was to keep me out of mischief. How sharply printed on the clean page of memory are the events of that glorious time! He called me his 'Ganymede,' and each day after the midday meal I brought his glass of 'shrub' and filled his yard-long Turkish pipe with shag and aniseed, and when he slept I spread the gaudy, gossamer bandana over his ruddy face and kept silence till he awoke. How well I remember climbing up the ladder at the side into the square 'cot' that hung, by many converging strands of whipcord, like the ribs of a fan, to the garret roof, and the gladness of being awakened in the early mornings by the music of the birds or by the resounding note of the village blacksmith's hammer upon his anvil. The smithy was not far off, and dearly I loved to visit it and see the Allisons, father and son—handsome they were both and stalwart—shower their strokes in rapid patter on the white-hot bar that splashed out fiery rain; and then the carpenter's shop, of which I had the run, and where I learnt to use the plane, the mallet, and the chisel, and at the same time to cut and hammer my half-grown fingers. I was an inquisitive boy, with already a wide general interest in things. I knew from observation how horses were shod, cows milked, how grass was cut, hay made and stacked, and how the wheat harvest was gathered in. I can still recall the

---

[1] The boys in order of age were: John, Joseph, George, and Alfred. The girls were: Elizabeth, Isabella, Mary Jane, and Emma.

remonstrant tone of Farmer Lee's voice as, following the line of reapers—women and men—with sickles, he reiterated the formula, ' Shear law doon,' ' shear law doon,'—and the feast that followed; the *melle*, with *gisor* and dance of ·young men and maids. Then, further afield, I knew the haunts of birds and where they built their nests, the structure of them, and the colour and markings of their eggs. I knew the flowery banks hard by the sea, and the sweet smell of the spring fields, yellow with primroses and cowslips—the hedges white with may that later blushed with the wild rose.

" I knew the tailor's and the cobbler's arts so far as these can be known by early and careful observation. I knew, too, how nails were made, and candles, for had I not almost every day, coming from school—or oftener, going to it—seen, through his open window, the chandler dipping the balanced frame, from which the wicks hung, into the melted, bad-smelling fat ? And had I not with equal frequency stopped and made long inspection of the process that transformed the iron bars into nails of many different sizes and kinds ? I was already so far acquainted with technical industry. But that is not by far the measure of my boyish knowledge of these common, but not always observed, everyday forms of handicraft. Perhaps the reason was that up to the time of going to school I was allowed much liberty; I roamed about with my elder brother, John, and we did not shut our eyes except in sleep. In these wayward excursions I had seen lime kilns, and a factory for making crucibles. I can remember, from the time I was four years old, how lime was made—and within a year or two I had been in a Deptford glass house and seen the red-hot ' metal' twirled about at the end of a long tube, blown into and rolled and shaped into a bottle, and seen a spiral twisted stick made and a coachman's whip, and came away the happy possessor. I had seen the inside of a pottery more than once, and had watched the working of the potter's wheel and the making of cups and saucers ; knew how they were kept apart in the kiln, and had been in the tunnel groove where the clay was found. I had paid clandestine visits to a copperas works, where the green sparkle of the crystal crust that lined the great square pits astonished and delighted. I knew the brick field, and had watched often and long the draggled women carrying the bricks from the moulding table, had watched the piling of the great stack of dried bricks with sprinkling of fine cinder between the layers.

" I knew how hemp was heckled and spun into rope yarn, and how this was made into ships' cables, also the virtues of Stockholm tar and the serving mallet. One of my uncles being a rope-maker, I had the run of his rope walk until the rope walk was abandoned for a patent ropery, and with that change my experience of the art and mystery of rope-making was enlarged. There I made my first acquaintance with boilers and steam engines, with corn-milling, for there was an adjacent corn-mill, and with gas-making. Gas was made for the use of the factory, and I therefore had the advantage of seeing a complete gas-making plant on a small scale. On Queen Victoria's Coronation Day these same gasworks supplied the gas for the first gas illumination I ever saw, a great V.R. in hundreds of flickering jets ; and this was not my uncle's only contribution to the tokens of rejoicing on that day, for I saw several of his tar barrels sent blazing down the High Street. But that was not a voluntary contribution ; the tar barrels were stolen.

" The same uncle, Robert Cameron, was an inventor as well as a rope-maker, and I believe was awarded a prize for an improved lifeboat. He also made improvements in rope-making machinery.

" My education was, according to common rule, rather neglected ; but I owe very much of my true education to that neglect (I was very much let alone, and allowed to roam about and see what I could). But presently the conventions had to be to some extent regarded, if not rigidly observed, and I was sent to school, a dame school,

B

kept by three dear old ladies, the Misses Herries. They were sisters ; their father lived with them and seemed no older than they. They were to me all about the same age, and all old; 'decayed gentlefolk' some might have called them. I seldom saw the old gentleman, but once I vividly remember his coming into the schoolroom, where I was sitting on a low form wrestling with a *primer*, for he made an imposing figure in a long dressing-gown. He had come to show the children a very wonderful thing, a glass prism, and how, when the sunbeam was caught upon it, a rainbow was made on the wall behind. That was my first intentional lesson in physics, and I shall never forget it nor the strange pleasure it gave me. At this school I stayed perhaps a year or two, and there I learnt several useful accomplishments. I learnt not only to spell and read stumblingly, but to darn a stocking neatly, to knit and to hem and use the needle in making several other kinds of stitches: the running stitch, the herring-bone, the buttonhole and sampler, the whole alphabet in stitches with ' etc.' at the end, and, outside the lettered square, 'a border phantasy of branch and flower and yellow-throated nestlings of the nest.'

" It was about this time that I made my first acquaintance with electrical phenomena, produced by the electrical machine.

" Mr. John Ridley, a friend of our family, was possessor of an electrical machine and such apparatus as generally accompanied it for experiments at the time—the insulating stool, the Leyden jar, the discharging rods, and a festoon of brass chain. I was greatly entertained and, more than that, astonished and deeply interested in the experiments Mr. Ridley showed me, and naturally the desire was created to possess an electrical machine ; and this desire was kept alive and stimulated by not infrequent repetitions of Mr. Ridley's experiments. I was able to satisfy this desire completely very soon after I left school. Mr. Ridley afterwards distinguished himself as the inventor of a reaping machine largely used in Australia.

" My brother John had been sent to a large boys' school kept by a Dr. Wood at Hendon Lodge, and after a short interval, during which I had been advanced to a higher grade of dame school, I joined him there, very glad of the reunion, for we were always inseparable companions whenever there was opportunity. We called each other Castor and Pollux. My entrance, therefore, into the boys' schoolroom was made under the ægis of my brother. It was a large school of about 200 boys. Hendon Lodge was a large old country mansion, with extensive grounds that afforded ample scope for boys' games. I suppose I was here for about two years, after which time the school was removed to Hylton Castle, which stands in the country, about two miles on the north side of the river from Sunderland. Hylton Castle is chiefly known for its ghost, ' The Cauld Lad of Hylton,' a servant-man murdered in a fit of passion by his master, one of the Barons of Hylton.

" I remember, as one of the notable school incidents occurring before the removal of the school to Hylton Castle, that Dr. Wood made a proclamation to the school-boys as follows :

" ' Now, boys, if any of you want to write letters, I want to tell you that from to-morrow you can send a letter from one end of the country to the other, from Land's End to John o' Groat's house, all the way for a penny.'

" My brother and I left school together, he being fourteen and I not thirteen. Our scholarly equipment was therefore not extensive. Still I think it was not so much what I learnt at school as what I spontaneously absorbed out of school hours, by keeping my eyes and ears wide open and cogitating a good deal over what I saw and heard or was doing. I did not then read very much, but that which took my fancy I not merely read but remembered.

" We had the advantage of good school-books. Among these was a book I made full use of : *Ewing's Elements of Elocution.* This book contained many examples of good literature, both prose and verse, and I owe very much of my love for poetry to the happy introduction which this book gave me to it. Then there was another school-book of quite an exceptional character. It was a little book of rudimentary chemistry, written by Hugo Reid at an eventful period of chemical history, which had a great influence on the bent of my mind. It gave in a very clear way an account of the then newly-ascertained facts which established Dalton's atomic theory, and was illustrated with drawings of apparatus necessary to perform the experiments described. It made me acquainted for the first time with the manipulation of laboratory apparatus, incidental to the generation and storage of gases. I am afraid that the elements of curiosity and sensational effect were at this time the strongest motives in the choice of particular experiments in the field of chemistry, and that perhaps pyrotechny would more accurately describe their character.

" I had already learnt what were the constituents of gunpowder, and most of its properties, and had had experience of the facility with which one could hurt oneself with it. Having the good fortune to have access to a quite considerable store of the raw material, in the bottles and drawers of a very kind and indulgent relative who was a druggist, I naturally availed myself of the advantage, and with the result of very material additions to my acquaintance with the technology of gunpowder-making and explosions."

About this time the family fortunes, which had been gradually waning, were at a low ebb. Chiefly through the father's too generous and easy disposition, which led him to assist any friends in difficulties by backing their bills and to consider the interests of his workpeople before his own, and also through a propensity to launch out in too many directions, he was less and less able to support his large family. As his means decreased, the burden of household expenses fell more and more heavily on his wife and eldest daughter Elizabeth, who, being some years older than her brothers and sisters, was almost like a younger sister to her mother. Large-hearted and wise, she was a natural bearer of the burdens of others, and she shared with her parents a complete knowledge of the family difficulties, and worked literally day and night to overcome them.

Her mother—though a slender, delicate woman of middle age—was strenuous and capable, and combined thriftiness with the ability to make the necessary privations and economies acceptable. In order to supplement the family income, she and Elizabeth started a little school for girls, which prospered and provided a regular contribution to meet household expenses.

After leaving school Joseph Swan went for a while to Elwick to stay with his great-uncle, Captain Kirtley, who had taken a most fatherly interest in the boy's future. In the autumn of 1842 he returned to Sunderland, and following out the idea which appealed to him, no less than to his parents, as a suitable scheme of life —suitable, that is, as a means of earning a livelihood and at the same time indulging a natural bent—he was articled as an apprentice to a Sunderland firm of druggists, Hudson & Osbaldiston. The term prescribed by this arrangement was that he should serve six years ; but as both the principals in this firm died within the first three years, he became free, and took advantage of the opportunity to join his friend John Mawson in his business of chemist and druggist at Newcastle.

These three years of his life, spent as a druggist's apprentice in Sunderland, although for the most part devoted to the most commonplace duties such as fall to the lot of an apprentice, yet were by no means barren of opportunities and educational advantages, which had a distinct and useful bearing upon his future career. He became a member of the Sunderland Athenæum and gained access to a good library which contained some scientific books and the scientific journals of the day.

Among these were *The Edinburgh and Dublin Philosophical Magazine* and a then quite new publication, *The Electrical Magazine*, edited by C. V. Walker. He also browsed through the *Repertory of Patent Inventions*, and recalls reading in this publication an account of J. W. Starr's incandescent electric lamp. This lamp, patented in England in 1845,[1] consisted of a short carbon pencil operating in a vacuum above a column of mercury. Several of these lamps were exhibited in London, but they were not a commercial success, as they blackened very rapidly. Nevertheless, the lamp of this young American inventor may justly be regarded as the prototype and first real contribution to the evolution of the incandescent as distinct from the arc type of electric lamp.

There were also not infrequent lectures on scientific subjects, chiefly relating to electricity and chemistry. It was in connection with these that Joseph Swan first became acquainted with the apparatus and manipulation connected with the production of electric light.

W. E. Staite had invented a "regulator lamp," by means of which he obtained some approach to constancy of the arc light, produced between rods of carbon, and he had employed a member of the Carland family (a well-known Sunderland family of clock- and watch-makers) to contruct his lamp.

There were other connections of a business kind between Staite and Sunderland which led this inventor to visit the town several times and repeatedly to deliver lectures there. Sir Joseph Swan has left some record of these lectures.

"I heard him lecture," he says, "several times at Sunderland, and saw all his apparatus. I also heard him, in later years, lecture at Newcastle and Carlisle. I remember that in addition to showing his lamp, which it was the principal object of his lecture to exhibit and which he proposed should be utilized immediately for lighthouse purposes, he also on one occasion, in the

---

[1] Under the name of E. A. King, his attorney.

Athenæum at Sunderland, illustrated the principle of electric lighting by means of a piece of iridio-platinum wire. Besides this, I saw this principle very well illustrated at Richardson's lectures at the same place. This arrested my attention and led me to ponder the question, even at this early period, how to produce electric light on this principle, but so as to avoid the use of a fusible wire. It was something like a seed sown in my mind, which germinated."

There are other fragmentary records of this period which may be quoted.

" During these three years," he writes, " all my spare time was spent in chemical and electrical experiments, carried out for the most part by means of home-made apparatus and appliances. I do not know whether it is a general experience or happy chance helping me, but somehow I have always been able to utilize, in my experimental work, things that happened to be well within my reach and that seemed to offer themselves to me.

" Daniell's battery had lately been invented, and with it and through it came the discovery of the art of electrotype which developed into electroplating, and eventually expanded into the great and varied industry of electrometallurgy. I well remember my first contact with it and with what delight it affected me. A neighbouring wood-turner, one Walker, whose workshop was not a stone's throw from me, came one morning for a pound of sulphate of copper. He brought in his hand a large medallion of the head of Napoleon (I think by David) in copper—a really fine electrotype. He explained to me the astonishingly simple way in which he had produced this, using a piece of zinc in a tree-pot with acid, and, on the outside, the sulphate of copper solution dissolved in similar acid. From that moment I became an electrotypist and did a great deal of work experimenting in this line, much helped in this by a capital little hand-book on electrotype manipulation by C. V. Walker.

" I pursued electrotyping with considerable avidity and success, and had several acquaintances much older than myself who were also devotees of the art ; and I was stimulated and helped by co-operation with them. This work, of course, led directly to acquaintance with and construction of all the various kinds of voltaic cell, such as the Daniell, Grove, and Smee, which had a little before that time been invented and come into vogue in connection with electrical experiments. I also became well acquainted with the modifications of the Grove battery which Staite made use of, namely, the Callan and Bunsen batteries.

" It was a remarkable time in the way of scientific invention. I recall, for example, that it was then that I first had my imagination kindled in a new direction. As I passed the shop window of Thomas Robson, a well-known engraver in Bridge Street, Sunderland, I had there my first glimpse of a photographic portrait. It was a most excellent daguerreotype portrait of Mr. Robson. I paid repeated visits to that window, while it hung there, with constantly increasing wonder at this astounding scientific achievement. I had heard of the conjuror's hoax of your likeness seen in a mirror, fixed there by a process of baking. Here was fiction turned to fact, a miracle realized. Here was a rival of electrotype in the inclination of my thoughts and the employment of my spare time. The ambition to pursue photography, however, had to wait for its fulfilment to a slightly later time, though it was seldom out of my thoughts. Involuntarily it connected itself in my mind with electrotyping.

" Photography from this moment became a popular art like electrotyping, at least to such an extent as to induce the publication of hand-books of the same type as that to which I have referred. Presently there issued from the same source *Daguerreotype Manipulation*, by Bingham, and through it I was informed of the possibility of reproducing a daguerreotype by electrotyping, which showed with not quite the brilliancy of the original, but with surprising clearness, all the fine detail of the daguerreotype picture.

"I feel strongly that acquaintance with these newly-discovered arts from the time of their birth greatly added to their impressiveness, giving them a vivid interest which those who have only been acquainted with them after they have attained a certain maturity and become common knowledge altogether missed. The elation created by the announcement of a great discovery and first acquaintance with its results is a sensation of an extraordinarily uplifting character, and I can never forget its effect as a stimulus to experimental effort."

CHAPTER II

IT was in 1846 that Joseph Swan, then a lad of eighteen, went to Newcastle to join his friend and future brother-in-law, John Mawson, who had left Sunderland and started a chemist's business on the "Side." [1] This business was afterwards removed to Mosley Street, and ultimately became the well-known firm of "Mawson & Swan."

John Mawson was a man of mark. He combined with a strong and straightforward character a singularly attractive personality. It was said of him that wherever he went he made friends. The only enemy he had, confessed—after the tragic accident that ended John Mawson's life—that his ill-will had been due to envy of one so universally beloved. His success in life was the reward of his sterling qualities. Whilst quite a young man he had become surety for a friend, on whose default he became primarily liable for heavy debts. Being unable to discharge these at that time, he was made bankrupt; later on he paid all the creditors in full. This honourable action won him universal esteem and confidence, and thus laid the foundations of his prosperity in business and of his civic position, for he was Sheriff of Newcastle at the time of his death.

Joseph Swan was fortunate in his association with such a man; and John Mawson was no less fortunate in his young assistant. He took a lively interest in Swan's ideas, and employed him as little as possible in irksome tasks, setting him free to follow his own bent for scientific researches. This policy proved quite a successful one for the business, for Swan soon became known as a helpful consultant to such Tyneside men as were interested in science, more especially in photography, and to

---

[1] A steep street of the city, containing at that time a number of quaint Elizabethan houses.

the chemical manufacturers who required technical advice about their work; and through this connection he gradually enlarged the scope of the business. Dispensing had been added to the sale of drugs and chemicals, and, before long, Swan began the manufacture of the collodion for which his firm quickly became famous.

On his removal to Newcastle, Swan parted company, of necessity, with the coterie of kindred spirits in Sunderland who shared his youthful interest in scientific experimentation, but at Newcastle he soon found other scientifically-minded friends, and two in particular who were in full sympathy with him and altogether after his own heart. They were John Pattinson and Barnard Simpson Proctor.

John Pattinson was an analytical chemist at the Felling Chemical Works, in which Hugh Lee Pattinson, F.R.S., well-known as the discoverer of the lead desilverizing process called by his name, was a principal partner. In the same works, closely associated with Mr. Pattinson, was John Glover, distinguished as the inventor of the Glover tower, widely used in the concentration of sulphuric acid.

Barnard Proctor was a pharmaceutical chemist, who in later life became the author of a book on pharmacy, and the professor of Pharmacy in the Newcastle College of Science. He had the further distinction of being a nephew of Michael Faraday. These three young men constituted themselves into a small scientific society, to which, perhaps as much in satire as in appreciation, their friends awarded the style of " The Three Philosophers."

Weekly meetings were held at each of their homes in turn for the discussion of scientific questions. These meetings generally wound up with music, of which all three were fond and to which all were able to contribute in some measure; more especially John Pattinson, who was a very fine amateur musician. Swan has himself recorded some of the activities of this philosophical trio.

" On holidays we visited chemical works together. The subjects discussed at our meetings were chiefly connected with the chemical work we had been doing incidentally to our employment. I frequently had something to say of what I was doing in connection with the construction of electrical apparatus, for I had added a new branch of chemical and other scientific apparatus to Mr. Mawson's business, and in leisure time was doing experimental work both in connection with electricity and photography.

" At several of the meetings I discussed with my colleagues the subject of electric lighting, and exhibited to them the results of my experiments in the production of carbon filaments made with a view to incandescent electric lighting. These chiefly consisted of narrow strips of paper of various kinds, which I had carbonized in such a way as entirely to prevent the oxidizing action of the air upon them, by surrounding them completely in a sufficiently thick wall of charcoal powder and heating them to a very high temperature in the biscuit kiln of a pottery. The smaller experiments were made in crucibles and the larger in saggars."

A fuller account of these early experiments and their sequel will fall more fitly into a later chapter, which deals more particularly with Swan's invention of the incandescent electric lamp.

During his first few years in Newcastle he lived with his grandmother, Mrs. Cameron, in Saville Row. Later on, after John Mawson's marriage with Elizabeth, the eldest daughter, Joseph rejoined the Swan household. The family had at that date migrated from Sunderland, giving up the little school there, and had established itself for a while in Newcastle at a house in Northumberland Street, moving later to Bloomfield Terrace at Gateshead. Things began to go better with them. All the sons were doing work of some kind. John was acting as dispenser at the Homeopathic Dispensary; Joseph was taken into partnership with his brother-in-law, John Mawson; George had gone to New Zealand to take up a business career; and Alfred was

JOSEPH WILSON SWAN AT THE AGE OF 21

studying architecture. There were three daughters left at home. With all these young people in the house there was no lack of liveliness and variety of interest.

It was a time when there was passing through Europe a great wave of revolutionary thought and action, which appealed to many young and generous minds. John and Joseph and some of their friends were advanced Liberals in politics, and even went so far as to start a small revolutionary paper which, however, was a short-lived affair. But their interest in Liberal causes continued, and the revolutionary and liberty movement in Italy, championed by Mazzini and Garibaldi, met with their warm sympathy.[1] This was stimulated by meeting various members of the Young Italy party who frequented Sir Joseph Cowen's house at Blaydon. Felice Orsini, who stayed there after his escape from an Austrian prison, and whose romantic adventures and strikingly handsome person and beautiful voice captivated them, became one of their heroes, till his attempt on the life of the Emperor Napoleon III., in 1858, brought his life to a miserable end.

But Joseph Swan had little time to spare for political activities. The all-absorbing preoccupation for his spare time was always his experimental work.

The decade which followed his successful establishment of the manufacture of photographic collodion, in 1856, as a branch of John Mawson's business, was mainly devoted to the study and trial of newly-discovered photographic processes and to the testing of his own ideas for the improvement of published methods or the devising of some novel applications of such processes to other purposes of practical use.

In the photographic studio which had been built at the top of the Mosley Street shop he worked late into the night, frequently helped by a keenly-interested

[1] John Swan and some of his friends joined in the presentation of a sword of honour to Garibaldi on one of his visits to the north of England.

apprentice, Thomas Barclay,[1] destined himself one day to found a highly successful business of a similar kind.

It was during this period that Swan's attention was focused more particularly upon the problem of producing permanent photographic prints ; photographs, that is, that were free from the defect of fading. This line of experimentation eventuated, in 1864, in his invention of the process of photographic printing known as the " carbon process."

In speaking of his invention of the " carbon process," as also in speaking of his other inventions, it is perhaps expedient and convenient at this point to guard against a possible misconception. It rarely, if ever, happens that any invention can be credited wholly and exclusively to one inventor. Swan was always most prompt and generous in acknowledging the work of other inventors. " There are no inventions," he was wont to say, " without a pedigree." Critically examined and analysed, an invention is seen to be a derivative and composite thing, the result of successive and progressive accretions of knowledge. It may seem invidious, therefore, to single out any one person alone for the credit of an invention such as the "carbon process" or the incandescent electric lamp. From the practical point of view, however, the essential requirement of an invention is its utility. In a certain sense no invention which involves an addition to previously existing knowledge can be said to be wholly useless. The failures of unsuccessful inventors often make admirable stepping-stones for those who come after. Nevertheless, an invention which fails to achieve the purpose for which it is designed, and so fails to provide the public with any useful addition to existing appliances (other than a " stepping-stone ") sinks not unnaturally into comparative oblivion, and it is the later experimenter, shrewdly perceiving the cause of failure in

---

[1] Afterwards Sir Thomas Barclay, a noted chemical manufacturer of Birmingham, and one of the pioneers of the scheme for bringing Welsh water to Birmingham.

the work of his predecessors, and ingeniously discovering and providing the necessary additions or corrections to remedy the defect, who is usually and fairly entitled to the credit of the invention.

And so it was with the " carbon process " of photographic printing. There were many experimenters, notably a French inventor, M. Alphonse Poitevin, who devised and described processes of carbon printing ; but none of these attained any degree of success, though many of them contributed new knowledge which materially assisted in the development of the art. Swan it was who succeeded, by the introduction of important modifications in previous methods, in devising a " carbon process " which was not only in itself eminently successful technically, but won a wide popularity, so that the expression " carbon process " became the recognized and distinctive description of *his* " carbon process."

The particulars of the development of this important invention and of his kindred photographic inventions are reserved for the chapter which immediately follows.

Some of the experiments upon which he was engaged at the commencement of this period involved a considerable exposure to corrosive chemical fumes. It was most likely from this cause that he contracted, in 1855–6, a serious affection of the lungs. To recover his health he was sent with his sisters to Rothesay, in the Isle of Bute, where in the pure soft air of the west coast his lungs healed, and he found strength to resume his work.

During these years he had become acquainted with two sisters, Maria and Mary White, who on the death of their father, a Liverpool merchant, had come to Newcastle to engage in a business owned by a cousin of John Mawson. Through them he came to know another sister, Fanny, a girl of vivacious and affectionate nature, with a keen sense of humour. She was a teacher in an excellent school where she had been a pupil. This school, which was first at Liverpool and then at Champion Hill, Streatham, belonged to Miss Thornley, a large-hearted woman with sound ideas of education in advance of those of her time. Her relations with Miss Thornley were almost those of daughter and mother. On her visits to her sisters in Newcastle she and Joseph Swan found themselves so much in sympathy that, in 1861, they became engaged, and in July 1862, they were married at Camberwell Chapel from Miss Thornley's house. After a honeymoon spent in the Isle of Wight, they returned to the north to a small house in Normanby Terrace at Gateshead.

In 1863 a son, Cameron, was born, and in 1864 a daughter, Mary Edmonds. The house then being too small for the growing family, a move was made to 21 Leazes Terrace, Newcastle, and here, in April 1866, Joseph Henry was born.

Swan's thoughts and energies at this time were closely engaged in scientific problems of various kinds, more particularly in those connected with the perfection of the carbon process, to which passing reference has already been made. In connection with the sale of the foreign patent rights in this invention, Swan paid his first visit to the Continent in July 1867. Accompanied by his wife, he managed to combine with business a good deal of pleasant sight-seeing in Germany, Switzerland, and France.

At the end of the year twin boys were born, and then came sorrow upon sorrow.

Just about this time a large quantity of nitro-glycerine was discovered in a stable in Newcastle. The origin of the deposit of this high explosive was never ascertained. The question of its removal and safe disposal was discussed at the Town Council. It was suggested at first that it should be thrown into the river, but on further consideration it was deemed safer to have it carted to the Town Moor and buried there in one of the " creeps " or gullies. John Mawson, who at that time was Sheriff of Newcastle, went with the carters in order to secure the careful handling of the explosive. But owing to some mishandling or misadventure the material exploded with terrific violence, killing outright or fatally injuring John Mawson and all who were assisting him.

The shock and sorrow caused by this tragic event were intense. On no one, save his wife and children, did the blow of John Mawson's death fall more heavily than on his partner and friend, who was almost immediately called upon to bear a still more crushing loss in the death of his own wife after a very short illness, in great measure attributable to the shock of hearing of John Mawson's death.

These successive calamities placed a greatly increased burden of responsibility on Swan's shoulders, taxing his strength to the utmost.

In addition to his usual scientific work and the heavy operation of making collodion, he had to undertake the entire management of the Mosley Street business. One of the first things he did on assuming control was to make his widowed sister Elizabeth Mawson a partner, thus securing to her the income that she would have enjoyed had her husband lived, and providing a practical interest for her in years to come.

CHAPTER III

THE CARBON PROCESS AND OTHER PHOTOGRAPHIC INVENTIONS

At an early date Swan's scientific curiosity had been aroused by the discoveries of Daguerre, Fox Talbot, Poitevin, and the other pioneers of the then new art of photography. He recalls that his first essay in photography was prompted by reading in a weekly journal of that day, *The Magazine of Science and Art*, an account of a new photographic process devised by Mungo Ponton, the essential materials of which consisted in a sheet of paper that had been sensitized in a solution of bichromate of potash. This was exposed under a flower or leaf or piece of lace to the action of sunlight in one of the transparent tracing-slates popular with children in those days. After exposure, the sheet was simply washed in water, which left a white and sometimes beautifully shaded silhouette of the semi-transparent object.

The chemical principle which underlies this simple process was one which the young experimenter was not slow to grasp; and having grasped it, it became for him an idea pregnant with possibilities, the starting-point for further developments and new applications, and he turned his thoughts keenly to the task of improving upon the methods then in vogue for obtaining photographic negatives and permanent prints from such negatives.

He read with the eagerness of an enthusiast all that was published in the technical papers concerning new photographic processes, and when, in 1851, Scott Archer published his discovery of the collodion process,[1] he was already prepared to follow up that great advance. The most essential and critical element in Archer's process

---

[1] The employment of collodion for photographic purposes was first suggested by Le Gray, but William Scott Archer was the first to make a really practical use of the discovery.

was gun-cotton (pyroxylin), the preparation of which had been to Swan a familiar art almost from the moment of its discovery. Without delay he commenced to manufacture collodion in Newcastle, making use of original methods and refinements which enabled him to produce it in a condition of extreme purity and uniformity. The formula which formed the basis of the manufacture, established by him in 1856, has been adhered to without material modification ever since, and is still in use at the present time. Its soundness is well attested by the fact that the bulk of the collodion used in this country for photographic purposes at the present day is produced according to this self-same formula settled over seventy years ago.

To trace the part which he played in the development of the process, originally known as the " carbon process " and in more recent times as the " autotype process," requires a brief retrospect.

In 1839 Mungo Ponton had shown how to produce images by the action of light on paper which had been impregnated with a solution of bichromate of potash. M. Edmond Becquerel, the distinguished French physicist, shortly afterwards diagnosed this phenomenon correctly in attributing it to the chemical reaction which took place between the chromic acid and the sizing in the paper. He discovered, in other words, that wherever the light acted upon the paper, it had, by reducing the chromic salt to the chromous condition, caused the size in the paper to become insoluble, so that upon subsequent washing the size was dissolved away in those parts of the paper upon which the light had *not* acted, but remained wherever the light *had* acted.

In 1852 Fox Talbot patented a method of photo-engraving in which he made use of this reaction between chromic acid and gelatine as a means of getting what is known as a " variable resist "—that is to say, a film of gelatine spread over a metal plate, which film, according to its greater or lesser thickness, offered a greater or lesser resistance to the attack of the etching acid. This, though not directly connected with the development of the carbon process, was in fact the first important practical application of the principle underlying Mungo Ponton's process, and naturally, therefore, called attention to it afresh and gave an added stimulus to those who were still experimenting with it.

Then in 1855 came the notable discovery and announcement by M. Alphonse Poitevin of the principles upon which carbon printing is based. M. Poitevin's idea was to render the reaction between chromic acid and gelatine available in producing photographs in permanent pigments. The process he adopted consisted in mixing a pigment with gelatine and chromic salt, and applying the mixture to paper. After exposure under a negative, the soluble portions were removed by washing, leaving an image formed by the colouring matter imprisoned in the insoluble gelatine.

M. Poitevin's attempt to produce a photographic print in the manner described was followed by a number of similar proposals put forward by a variety of inventors.[1] But all these suggested processes had this signal defect, which characterized also M. Poitevin's original invention: the pictures so produced were lacking in a perfect gradation of tone from light to dark. The reason of this (though not fully appreciated at that time) was as follows: where the light fell upon the gelatine film with full intensity, it rendered it insoluble all through its thickness. But where the light was partially obscured by the negative, only the surface skin of the gelatine film was acted upon and rendered insoluble, the thickness of this insoluble surface-layer depending upon the degree to which the light had penetrated into the body of the film. In the process of washing, in order to remove the still soluble parts of the film, the water first dissolves those portions of the film on which the light has not acted at

[1] Amongst Englishmen, Mr. Pouncy's name should be mentioned as an early experimenter in carbon printing.

all, and, wherever it is able, it penetrates laterally under the surface of the thin skin covering those parts of the film only partially acted upon. But it is obvious that there may be many such parts so isolated by completely insoluble gelatine that the water cannot get at them at all. Conversely, wherever there are parts completely surrounded by soluble gelatine, those parts will be entirely washed away, even though coated with a skin of insoluble gelatine. The result was that pictures produced in this way were harsh and inaccurate in their tone-gradation, and, in short, the process was not a practical success.

Towards the end of 1858 Swan commenced to experiment with the carbon process. He saw in the principle of this reaction great possibilities, in particular the possibility of forming relief pictures whose surface contour would perfectly correspond to the lights and shades of a silver print. Fully acquainted with the work that had already been done, he speedily came to the conclusion that the failure in the results hitherto attained arose from causes indicated above, and that these defects would be avoided if means could be devised for exposing to the action of the water *the side of the film remote from that which had been exposed to the action of light.*

His first attempt to carry out this idea consisted in coating a plate of glass with a mixture of lamp-black, solution of gum-arabic, and a solution of bichromate of potash. He exposed this plate, when dry, in a camera with the uncoated surface of the glass turned towards the light passing through the negative and lens. The plate was then washed with water, to remove from the back of the sensitive coating those portions of the film which the light had not rendered insoluble. The experiment, though right in principle, was not successful, probably through insufficient exposure ; and it was not until 1864 that he devised a satisfactory method of carrying this principle into effect.

The key to success consisted in making the sensitive

film a thing separate altogether from paper or only temporarily attached to paper during the initial stages of the operation.

In the simplest form of the process the first step is to produce from a coloured gelatinous solution a thin film or tissue of gelatine. The colouring matter was usually finely divided carbon, but it might be pigment or dye of any desired colour. This tissue is rendered sensitive with bichromate of potash. If desired, it may be strengthened with a temporary backing of paper which renders it easier to handle ; and this was in practice the usual method adopted. The tissue is then placed under a negative in an ordinary photographic printing-frame and exposed to light. After exposure, but before development, it is cemented, with the exposed surface downwards, to its permanent backing of paper or other material by means of a solution of india-rubber or other medium not soluble in water. The picture is then washed in warm water, which first removes the temporary paper backing and so obtains access to that side of the gelatine tissue remote from the side directly exposed to the light in the photographic frame.

The soluble portions of the tissue are then readily removed, leaving the picture formed by the insoluble portions adhering to the mount. In this way pictures were obtained which reproduced with exquisite delicacy and faithfulness the tone-gradations of the original. And the process itself, although the description sounds somewhat complicated, was in fact a simple one, and the results attained by it left nothing to be desired, either as regards quality or permanence. In reproducing a pencil, charcoal, or crayon drawing, the pigment used for staining the tissue could, if desired, be the actual colour and material used by the artist. Thus drawings in sepia, red chalk, indian ink, etc., could be reproduced in the veritable medium of the original.

Swan patented his carbon process in 1864.[1] This was

[1] Patent No. 503.

the first patent he ever took out; the forerunner of some seventy patented inventions which now appear under his name in the Patent Office Register. He drew the specification himself, and, though its interest is now mainly antiquarian, nevertheless it deserves to rank for the clearness of its scientific exposition and the thoroughness of its working instructions as a model of what a well-drawn patent specification should be.

The materials required for carrying out the carbon process, the most important of which was the carbon tissue, were few and simple, and were originally supplied by the firm of Mawson & Swan. Later on, the commercial utilization and development of the process on the broad lines, which its value as a means of procuring perfect and permanent reproductions of works of art warranted, were undertaken by the Autotype Company. This company acquired Swan's English patent rights and carried on the carbon process under the now familiar name of *Autotype*, whilst the Scottish rights were made over to Thomas Annan, a well-known photographer with studios and works at Lenzie, near Glasgow.

The foreign rights in the carbon process were purchased by Messrs. Braun of Dornach, in Alsace-Lorraine, by whom it was extensively used in reproducing many of the famous masterpieces in chalk and monochrome from the continental picture galleries.

The carbon process, important in itself, has had far-reaching effects upon cognate branches of photography. Employed for the purpose of producing a variable resist to the action of the etching fluid in photogravure, it is the parent of that most highly refined form of photo-mechanical reproduction; [1] but its use developed also in another direction. The greater or less relief, which characterizes in a carbon print the parts more or less acted upon by light, affords a means of forming a metallic impress or

---

[1] The use of the gelatine film of Swan's carbon process as a " resist " for etching through (an improvement on Fox Talbot's intaglio process) was brought to perfection by Herr Karl Klic of Vienna.

matrix by pressing the print into soft metal or by electrotype, and the prints yielded by means of a solution of coloured gelatine from such a matrix constitute, by a species of casting, facsimiles of the original carbon picture in coloured gelatine. This process, which is commonly known as *Woodbury-type*, reproduces, in a purely mechanical manner, and on the same principle, the shading of a carbon print, *i.e.*, by utilizing the difference in the thickness of the gelatine pellicle as the means of obtaining a corresponding depth of colour. Such prints or casts are particularly interesting as being products of a mechanical method of obtaining the characteristic qualities of a photograph and, at the same time, as an entirely new departure in processes of mechanical printing. Though developed and brought into commercial use by others, notably by W. Woodbury, the new principle of printing involved in this process was the invention of Swan.[1]

About this time he also devised and patented some modifications of the process referred to whereby an electrotype made from a granular carbon print was adapted to the ordinary process of intaglio copper-plate printing.[2] This method was employed and brought to a high state of perfection by a French firm, Boussod, Valledon et Cie. of Paris, and their successors, Messrs. Goupil et Cie., and was known as *Goupilgravure*.

The relief feature of the carbon picture has been taken advantage of in several other photo-mechanical printing processes as a means of obtaining pictorially equivalent light and shade in resulting prints. In one of these, by a combination of a photograph and ruling machine with attached cutting tool, a line-engraving closely corresponding to a woodcut is automatically produced. In one form or another the carbon process, as developed and rendered practicable by Swan in the manner described, has proved perhaps the most widely used of all the photographic processes of the present time, and has done

[1] See *Photographic News*, 1864, and Patent No. 1791 of 1865.
[2] Patent No. 239 of 1866.

more than any other to remove the reproach of " fading " from the photographic print, and to extend the use of photography in mechanical printing.

Many of the carbon prints made by Swan in 1864 still exist in perfect condition, as strong in tone as when they were made.

The half-tone processes for making typographic blocks, which are in use to-day for the illustration of books, magazines, and newspapers are also largely the outcome of his inventions. In his Patent No. 1791 of July 6th, 1865, he describes the method of making lined screens for photo-engraving, which is substantially that in use to-day, and in his Patent No. 2969, of July 22nd, 1879, he describes a most ingenious method of using such screens for producing " relievo " blocks for typographic printing, a method brought into commercial use by Messrs. Meisenbach two years later.

It was a characteristic of his mind that, whilst intent upon the objective primarily in view, he was always alert to perceive kindred applications for the novel phenomena which his experiments brought to light. Thus, in working out the carbon process, the observation of the indurating effect upon gelatine of the salts of chromic oxide (of which chrome alum is a type) at once suggested to him the application of this reaction to the leather-making industry as a means of toughening leather. He made special mention of this proposed use in the specification of a patent of his in 1866.[1]

" In tanning," states the specification, " I immerse the skins or hides in a solution of chromate or bichromate of potash or other suitable chromate or bichromate and I decompose the said chromate or bichromate in the skin or hide by means of oxalic or other suitable acid."

The discovery of the art of chrome tanning is usually attributed to Professor Knapp, who in 1858 in a German paper, and in 1861 in a British patent specification, proposes the treatment of hides and skins with " mixtures of

[1] Patent No. 330.

fatty or oily acids or mixtures of the same with metallic oxides such as oxides of iron, chromium, manganese." [1] Professor Knapp, however, seems himself to have regarded the use of the iron salts rather than the chromium salts as the important feature of his discovery. But the iron salts proved to be a failure. It is believed that Swan's announcement in the specification above-mentioned of the specific properties of the chrome salts in tanning leather is the first publication of this fact to be found in technical literature, and it is certain that his suggestion for using chrome salts for this purpose was made without any knowledge of Professor Knapp's publication, and was based entirely upon his own observations and experiments.

Although it is possible to produce chrome leather by the process described in Swan's patent, the strongly acid reaction of the reducing agent renders the process unsuitable for practical use. [2] It was not until 1878 that, by the mixture of alum with the chrome salt, Dr. Heinzerling brought the process of chrome tanning into commercial prominence.

Owing to the death of John Mawson in 1867, the whole business of the firm devolved upon the shoulders of the surviving partner, and for the next few years left him little leisure for research and experiment. But so far as the preoccupations of business permitted, his thoughts were still mainly focused upon improvements in photography.

Although reference at this point to his improvements in the photographic plate somewhat anticipates the strict chronological sequence of the narrative, it will nevertheless be convenient to allude here to the important advance which he made in this department of photography.

In 1871 Dr. R. L. Maddox proposed the use of gelatine in conjunction with bromide of silver as a

[1] Patent No. 2716 of 1861.
[2] See *Principles of Leather Manufacture*, by Prof. H. R. Proctor, D.Sc.

substitute for collodion for coating the glass plate, thus introducing the " dry " as distinct from the " wet " process of photography. But the gelatine dry plates, as at first made, were comparatively slow in their reaction to light ; moreover, the difficulty of their preparation, their lack of density, and the uncertainty of the results obtained with them, outweighed the advantages of a dry process; and, in fact, notwithstanding Dr. Maddox's publication, the wet collodion process was still the process most generally used.

Attracted to the subject by some very striking results obtained by the gelatino-bromide process, Swan in 1877 entered upon an experimental investigation with a view to remedy its defects. He so well succeeded in this object that in the latter part of the year his firm was supplying dry plates, which for the first time truly rivalled collodion in sensitiveness and in the general character of the image produced. At an early stage of this new manufacture he was led by annoying irregularities in the sensitiveness of the gelatino-bromide plate to examine into the cause, and as the result of a crucial experiment discovered that the difference in the behaviour of the plates was due to difference in the temperature at which the emulsion was prepared and to the length of time it was left hot. This discovery led to an immediate and great increase in the sensitiveness of the plates produced by his firm, and was in fact the real starting-point of the change that has made photography not only one of the most popular of amusements, but also one of the most important aids to scientific progress in many ways, particularly in connection with astronomical photography. Since he did not patent or publicly announce this discovery, but merely applied it in the manufacture in which he was engaged, he has not hitherto obtained the recognition to which he is entitled as the discoverer of the great accelerating effect of heat in the preparation of emulsions of gelatino-bromide of silver.

Amongst other photographic inventions which should be mentioned before leaving this domain of his work is the invention of " bromide printing paper," now in universal use, as a means of exceedingly rapid printing by artificial light.   Bromide paper was first proposed and patented by Swan in 1879.[1]

Although, as has been seen, he was mainly preoccupied with photographic researches for some years after the invention of the carbon process, his thoughts about this time became gradually concentrated upon speculations and experiments in another region of science with which his name is, perhaps, more generally or popularly associated, viz., electric lighting.   The genesis and development of the invention of the incandescent electric lamp will more fittingly form the subject of a separate chapter. But before passing on to this topic it is necessary to trace briefly some of the events which occurred during this period of his home life.

[1] Patent No. 2968.

CHAPTER IV

LOW FELL

FOR a year and a half after the death of his wife Swan stayed on in the house at Leazes Terrace with her sisters, Maria and Hannah, who had been with her at the time of her death, and remained to keep house and look after the elder children. The twin boys only survived their mother for a few months.

The heavy cares and responsibilities which followed upon the loss of his wife and his brother-in-law told upon his spirits and health. He suffered from a feeling of intense weariness. "My thoughts," he writes at this time, "stagnate and wander away in a vagrant manner almost without control, and I am left with a painful sense of having neglected to fulfil a duty." His mind constantly reverted to the past; his innate optimism seemed for a time daunted and his faith in the future to waver and fail.

In June 1869 came a much-needed respite from work in a holiday spent in the Lake District with a few congenial friends. John Hancock, the Northumbrian naturalist, a pupil of Thomas Bewick, was one of the party, and his intimate knowledge of birds and every form of wild life added much to the interest of their country rambles. Though not in the accepted sense of the word a naturalist, Swan was all through his life an intense lover of nature. The beauty of natural forms, colours and sounds at all times filled him with a pleasure akin to rapture. Professor John Tyndall, writing of Michael Faraday, remarks that "a thunderstorm and a sunset excited a kind of ecstasy in his mind." So it was with Swan. He delighted in the panorama of the sky, its pageant of clouds, its sunsets, the flash and thunderclap of its "high engendered battles." He loved the broad prospect of an English countryside seen from some favoured point of view, he loved the grandeur of mountain scenery and the impetuous rush of the waterfall. The shapes and foliage of trees, the colour and fragrance of flowers, the song of birds, the nightingale in particular, stirred his heart to deep emotion and seldom failed to bring to his lips some vivid word-picture from his favourite poets, Shakespeare and Tennyson. His letters abound with allusions to the sights and sounds of the country. In writing of a walk by Windermere during this holiday he speaks of " trees and flowers, light and shadow on the water, blue misty veils on the mountains, song of birds, a combination too beautiful. The tears came into my eyes more than once from the strong sense of it and its complicated associations."

In the summer of 1869 he was planning a move from Newcastle, and had taken a house at Low Fell, Gateshead. In July he writes, " We all live too much in the midst of smoke and anxieties. The one robs the body of its natural nourishment and the other the mind," and again, " The time has at last come when we must leave the old house marked by so many sad and joyful memories. I hardly know whether pain or pleasure prevails in leaving it." The new house, " Underhill," was a pleasant change from Newcastle. It stood under the High Fell and had a good garden looking across intervening corn fields towards the Ravensworth hillside and the valleys of the Teams and Tyne. Several other members of the family were by now settled at Low Fell, which was then a little village set among green fields,whose freshness was only marred here and there by the black machinery of a pit. The clannishness of the family then as always made it a joy for the different members to meet each other. Many and delightful were their gatherings, and the children of the different families grew up in happy comradeship.

About this time Swan's interest in national education was awakened. He writes on November 26, 1869, "I have just come in from a meeting held in the Mechanics' Institute to form a branch of the Birmingham Educational League. It was a most interesting meeting. I was greatly pleased with Mr. Collings of Birmingham.[1] He has a very large business, employs twenty-six clerks and six travellers, and yet has time to come here to stir up the dull spirit of our townspeople on this important question of national education, and he does it with great ability and an enthusiasm that is quite refreshing, an energy that drags one along with it. I greatly admire and envy the possession of this rare quality." His interest, thus aroused, led him, in spite of the double call of his business and his experiments, to become a member of the Gateshead School Board. He also later became a member of the Town Council of Gateshead, in each case using his influence to further a liberal and progressive policy.

During this period his experimental work proceeded slowly. His time was largely taken up with business, which left him little energy for work in the laboratory. He was also still feeling the effects of nervous strain. Though considerably refreshed by his holiday in the Lake Country, he at times complained of a feeling of inertia and weariness.

In November 1869 he writes to Hannah White, " The pain in my chest is quite gone, and I am quite well unless for a feeling of languor which troubles me. The worst of it is that experiments make no progress when this feeling is upon me. They have made little or no progress since you left, or almost none. Every day I think of them and wish for opportunity. I give you my promise that I will devote myself to them with more energy, and that right soon. Thank you for the stimulus of your words, I sadly need the urging."

But the will to work was not the only condition requisite for successful experimentation. A plentiful supply of sunshine was also an important element for the particular work in hand. In December he writes, alluding to his experiments in photo-engraving : " It is a serious drawback to business, this dull weather ; in most

---

[1] Jesse Collings, well-known advocate of free education and land reform.

of my work, you know, gas-light is inadmissible. I made
a failing attempt at the engraving experiments the other
evening; all went wrong, and I have not tried again.
To-morrow is Saturday and therefore a busy day, and not
for experimenting, and that is the end of another week.
I fear I shall be too late, for the prize is lying now quite
unearthed and ready to be picked up at any moment.
I wish I had more time and more energy."

A glass-house with a dark room for photographic work
had been built on to "Underhill," and from this time was
in constant use for experimental work. It was here that
some of his improvements in dry-plate photography were
evolved, and here that experiments with different processes of engraving were carried on, and, at a later period,
the making of the early filaments for the incandescent
electric lamp.

In the meantime the business of Mawson & Swan had
been growing and extending. The progressive instinct
of Swan led him to enlarge its scope by acquiring a
stationery and bookselling business, formerly carried on
by Marston of Grey Street. This expansion of the
business necessitated the taking of new premises, and the
relegation of the various activities of the firm to distinct
departments under separate management.

The stationery and bookselling department was placed
under the management of Thomas Morgan, a versatile
Irishman, who enlarged it by the addition of an art
gallery, in which famous modern pictures were exhibited
from time to time. For those were days in which
Newcastle possessed no public picture gallery.

The Mosley Street business, which dealt in scientific
apparatus and chemicals, was put into the charge of
James B. Payne, who also controlled the manufacture of
photographic plates and collodion, the latter a process
of great delicacy requiring constant personal supervision.
For many years Swan had kept the secret of this manufacture in his own possession. But as the calls upon his
time increased he was obliged to delegate this work.

In the choice of an assistant he was fortunate in selecting a man admirably fitted for this responsible task. The secret of the manufacture was faithfully guarded, and the process carefully supervised. The manufacture is now similarly carried on by his son, Arthur Payne.

Another branch of the business of Mawson & Swan was concerned with the importation of yeast. This business was first placed in the hands of Messrs. Blakey and Hurman, and subsequently entrusted to Sydney Carter, under whose able management it developed into an important trade.

Swan was at this time contemplating a great change in his life, namely, his marriage to Hannah White, who, with her sister Maria, had kept house for him and the children after his wife's death. Their devoted care had helped greatly to relieve and dispel the feeling of loneliness that had oppressed him since that bereavement.

The proposed union was a most natural and suitable one in spite of the existing state of the law with regard to marriage with a deceased wife's sister, which was then not legal in England, though a bill to legalize it was at that time in prospect. It also met with the approval of their respective relatives.

In a letter to Hannah White, December 7th, 1870, he writes, " It is a great pleasure to me that Emma and John (her sister and brother-in-law) approve of our union. I entirely agree with you that it will be wise to wait for the chance of the bill passing next year, but if it should not be brought into Parliament, or if it should be rejected, then let us not delay longer than the autumn."

No doubt in deciding upon this step he had also taken into consideration the future of the children. " The children are merry little companions," he writes, " beautifully good in temper and disposition. A heavy charge lies on me to keep them so, as far as the influence of circumstances can." The existing environment was a happy one, and he wished to keep it so ; and the step

D

he contemplated was best calculated to ensure its continuance.

Through all his letters of this time runs the thought of the children. Though so fully preoccupied with his experiments, he still found time to keep in close touch with them, entering into their games, suggesting and helping in the construction of new toys, to the making of which he would bring all his manipulative skill and all the varied resources of his laboratory. Now it was a miniature volcano which he helped them to construct, or a gigantic fire balloon ; at another time the amusement would be the production of an electrical snowstorm, or the blowing of soap bubbles of marvellous iridescence from a special mixture of his own compounding. As the children grew older he would read to them favourite passages from the *Canterbury Tales*, the *Idylls of the King*, and the *Day Dream*; or thrill them with a vivid recital of *Young Lochinvar*. So spirited was his performance of this ballad on one occasion that when he came to the words " he quaffed off the wine and he threw down the cup," he dashed to the ground, so tradition records, the tea-cup which he had taken up to suit more realistically the action to the word.

These are trivial memories, but it is only by little touches such as these that one can hope to give the impression of a father so delightful to his children. He was big and tender, simple and natural as a child, and original in his ways. He was amusingly absent-minded, particularly when he was pursuing some new idea. No one in his household expected an immediate reply to a casual question. The answer might come minutes afterwards, or even days. But though he might not appear to notice what was happening around him, very little in reality escaped his attention.

In the summer of 1871 " Underhill " was closed for a time owing to an outbreak of smallpox in the neighbourhood. The children and their aunts were sent to Moffat and to Keswick, while Swan, except for a short visit to the Lakes, remained in Gateshead, staying at "Ashfield," the home of the Mawson family.

A sunset, seen from Cat Bells during this visit, stirs him to rapture, and forms the theme of one of his letters. "It cannot be in any degree described;" he writes, "it was one of those things that one cannot half comprehend; the beauty seems infinite and one's capacity for receiving it painfully small. A sight always to be remembered with a sort of awe! At first the hill-tops were red hot; then the brightest glow slowly lessened and faded, and on one after another the light died out, and veils of grey mist most tenderly enfolded the more distant. The Borrowdale hills, rugged and picturesque in form, were thus obscured, and showed through a dreamy haze very beautiful and yet very mournful, as it seemed to me, for I fancied them as symbols of the past, growing more and more indistinct until the more distant vanished altogether."

The Bill for legalizing the marriage with a deceased wife's sister having failed to pass,[1] Joseph Swan and Hannah White decided to be married in Switzerland, a country in which such kinship was no bar to the legality of the marriage. Accordingly, on September 9th, 1871, Hannah White, with her sister Louisa as companion, set out for Switzerland, where her future husband was to join her later at Neuchâtel.

On September 29th he writes: "None of your letters have told me where I shall find you at Neuchâtel! I suppose you purpose meeting me at the station; but then I do not know precisely the hour of my arrival. You see 'Poste Restante' is the only address I have for you at Neuchâtel, and I cannot expect you to lie at the Post Office like a letter until I call for you."

The marriage took place at the Reformed Church in Neuchâtel on October 3rd, 1871. After a short stay in Switzerland they returned, staying in Paris on the way,

[1] Marriage with a deceased wife's sister was ultimately legalized by the Deceased Wife's Sister's Marriage Act, 1907.

where they saw the results of the siege and the damage done during the Commune. They were present at the trial of Rossel, one of the idealist leaders of the Communists.[1]

Then the busy, industrious life in the North was resumed. The marriage was a very happy one. In his wife he found a helpmate, cheerful, sympathetic, and understanding. She was of an energetic and practical temperament and had remarkable powers of organization. She took a great interest in her husband's experiments, learning the difficult art of photography, before dry plates, Kodak cameras and films made it an easy one. Her clever fingers helped in forming and packing up the filaments for mounting in the first electric lamp bulbs.

Between the years 1873 and 1880 five children were born: Hilda, Isobel, Kenneth, Percival, and Dorothy. The elder children were at school, except at holiday times.. They grew up as one family with her own, she doing everything she could to make them feel as little as possible the loss of their own mother. Her sister Maria remained with them, a much-loved and devoted member of the family, to the end of her long life.

In August 1876 Hannah Swan and the children went to Moss Hill, a farm-house at Milton near Carlisle, belonging to, but some miles away from the Tyndale Spelter Works, a property owned by a company chiefly composed of members of the Swan family, who used the house as a holiday resort for their children. It stood amid high meadows with an old-fashioned walled garden, sloping down to a dene, through which ran a burn. In the wide " lonnins " [2] between the fields grew wild roses and honeysuckle, ragged robin and water forget-me-nots. Beyond were fells and tarns and the lovely river Eden.

History and romance are bound up with that Border

---

[1] Rossel, with two other Communist leaders, Ferré and Bourgeois, was sentenced to death and shot on November 28th, 1871, at Satory, in the presence of 3000 soldiers.

[2] Cumberland dialect for " loaning," a lane or by-road.

country. The Roman Wall, with *fosse* and *vallum* clearly to be seen, runs for miles by the roadside from Lanercost to Bird Oswald (Amboglanna).

Lanercost Priory, where Edward I. lay dying, raging at his inability to carry on his warfare with the Scots, stands by the Eden, and near by is Naworth Castle, where the name of " Belted Will " leads the memory of Border warfare on to Tudor times. At the neighbouring town of Brampton, Prince Charlie received the keys of Carlisle from a kneeling deputation ; and on the Capon Tree, a mile away, some of his defeated followers paid the penalty for their loyalty to the Jacobite cause. The gravestone of Margaret Teesdale of Mump's Ha' (the original of Meg Merrilees) brings one to the later period described by Scott in *Guy Mannering*. The whole neighbourhood teems with tradition and interest to those who love to look into the past, while to eyes inured to the landscape of Tyneside, once so fair that John Wesley called it a " paradise on earth," but now seamed with collieries and seared with the smoke of chemical works, and sullied with the drab ugliness of mean streets, this Cumberland countryside was a revelation of fresh, unspoilt beauty.

In this happy hunting ground of Moss Hill Joseph Swan's wife and children spent many delightful summer months. But he himself was seldom able to come for longer than week-ends. At this time his attention was again concentrated upon the problem of producing an electric lamp by the incandescence of carbon in a vacuum.

Recent improvements in the Sprengel pump, enabling a far higher degree of evacuation to be attained than had previously been possible, opened up the prospect of overcoming the difficulties which had frustrated his earlier attempts in this direction. This improvement in the Sprengel pump coincided in point of time with a noticeable awakening of public interest in the possibilities of electric lighting. The years 1877–8 mark the commencement of this era. The daily Press, notably the *Times*, began to publish articles on the subject and to discuss the comparative merits of the various systems of electric lighting which were then for the first time tentatively competing for public favour.[1]

All these systems involved the principle of lighting by electric arc, a form of illumination well adapted for providing large centres of light, but not inherently suited for furnishing a number of small independent points of light. No one at this date had succeeded in supplying a practical solution for " the subdivision of the electric light," a phantom problem which loomed large in these days of series dynamos and arc lighting. Electricians were busily engaged in devising apparatus and systems of distribution to overcome this difficulty, for it was evident that until this problem was satisfactorily solved, electric lighting could not come into general use, at any rate for domestic illumination.

This growing demand for a scheme of electric lighting capable of giving small units of light acted, no doubt, as an incentive to Swan, convinced, as he was, that he possessed the key to the problem, and urged him to push on with his experiments.

He perceived that the solution of the problem lay not in complicated apparatus and systems for dividing and distributing the current, but in devising a practical form of electric lamp which was itself inherently suitable for attaining a subdivision of the light—a lamp which worked, not on the arc principle, but by the incandescence *in vacuo* of a thin continuous carbon conductor of high specific resistance, such as the films or filaments with which he had experimented intermittently for the past thirty years.

To diagnose the trouble and prescribe the right remedy was one thing, and Swan had already got a very clear and definite idea of what was needed in this regard, though there were many who failed to see in which direction the true solution lay, darkening counsel with many words and little knowledge. But it was quite

[1] See, for instance, *Times*, June 3rd and October 26th, 1878.

another thing to devise a commercially practical form of lamp fulfilling the prescribed conditions and capable of accomplishing the desired object. This, accordingly, was the problem to the solution of which Swan now directed his experiments with the utmost eagerness and intensity. In his concentration on this engrossing problem, sleep and meals were neglected and time was naught. Here it was that his wife, practical and punctual and orderly herself, was so admirable, not only in her patience with a disposition so different from her own, but in her active sympathy with his work.

Engrossing and urgent as was this experimental work upon the lamp, he could only afford to give at most a fraction of his time to it, for the business of Mawson & Swan still claimed the greater part of his attention. The manufacture of photographic dry plates, which had by this time outgrown the laboratory experimental stage, was added to the other activities of the firm and was carried on in a factory which had been specially built for the purpose at Low Fell.

In the autumn of 1878 an International Exhibition of Industry was held in Paris, comprising, as one of its most prominent features, an exhibit of various systems of electric arc lighting.

Swan, always keen to keep abreast of the latest developments, went over to Paris in November. He had an additional interest in this Exhibition owing to the fact that his firm was showing there an exhibit of pure chemicals, including pharmaceutical opium purified by a special process which he and Barnard Proctor had recently invented.[1]

London also, by this time, had its demonstrations of electric arc lighting. A letter written by Swan on his way to Paris reports a visit to the Gaiety Theatre to see the electric light.[2] " The effect is good," he writes,

[1] Patent No. 4765 of 1877.
[2] The lights shown in front of the Gaiety Theatre were operated on the Lontain system, a modified form of the Serrin arc lamp.

" but not by any means what is wanted for practical use. I am strongly inclined to give my plan for dividing the current to the public through the *Times*."

He was, as appears from this and many other letters, much tempted at this time to join in the general discussion of the problem of the " subdivision of the electric light," and publicly propound his own solution ; but he ultimately decided to defer any public announcement until he was in a position not only to prescribe the remedy but to provide the public with a practical lamp capable of being used in the manner prescribed.

In Paris he found that it was not only inside the Exhibition that the electric light was to be seen. The Place and Avenue de l'Opéra had a brilliant display of arc lights, whilst the Magasin du Louvre was glowing with no less than seventy lamps of the type known as " Jablochkoff candles." But his comment on all that Paris could show in the way of electric lighting was the same as his comment on the Gaiety display : " the effect was good, but much still remained to be done before electric lighting could be adopted for interior illumination." After a busy week of sightseeing in Paris, divided between the objects of interest within the Exhibition and those outside, he returned to resume his experiments in Newcastle.

CHAPTER V

THE common coupling of the name of Swan with that of Edison in connection with the incandescent electric lamp has often led to the notion that Swan collaborated with Edison in this invention. That was not so. Their work was entirely independent, and though each knew that the other was at work on the problem of devising a practical lamp, they never met or held any communication with each other. The conjunction of their names in this familiar linkage arose from the fusion in 1883 of the two competing companies formed to exploit Swan's and Edison's inventions respectively.

The successful transformation of the threatened rivalry of these competing concerns into a powerful organization under the name of the Edison and Swan United Electric Light Company has somewhat confused and clouded in the mind of the public the true view of the parts played by Swan and Edison respectively in the evolution of this notable invention. The perspective has been still further obscured, and even somewhat distorted, by the prolonged litigation upon which the company embarked for the purpose of establishing and maintaining its patent monopoly in the face of the widespread infringement which at the outset threatened to undermine it. The story of this great lawsuit is given in a later chapter.

In face of this confusion and in view of the somewhat pretentious and all-embracing claims which have from time to time been advanced on Edison's behalf by his over-zealous compatriots, it is very necessary that an accurate account of the facts should be placed on record. Amongst the scientific papers left by Swan is a full and detailed statement of these facts, showing from what early beginnings and by what gradual yet persevering steps he ultimately reached the desired goal.

The original statement is too long to quote *in extenso*.

It must suffice to reproduce the main features of the story.

It appears that his thoughts were first drawn to the subject of electric lighting by the lecture (to which allusion has already been made) delivered by Staite in the Sunderland Athenæum in 1845. Swan was then a lad of seventeen, and from that time onwards his mind was constantly recurring to this fascinating problem. Through the library of the Sunderland Athenæum he forthwith acquainted himself with every new electrical invention and idea bearing on the subject of electric lighting as soon as it was published. Significant and suggestive amongst these early publications was the patent specification of King, agent for J. W. Starr, a young American inventor, describing an apparatus for producing electric light by means of continuous metallic and carbon conductors in a Torricellian vacuum. This document was published in 1845, and has usually been cited as the first suggestion of an incandescent carbon lamp with carbon *in vacuo*.[1] Struck with the idea that by means of incandescent carbon *in vacuo* a useful form of lamp could be produced, Swan started at once to experiment in order to ascertain how to make an economical lamp on these lines. Even at this early date he realized the desirability of having the carbon conductor as thin as possible.

" It appeared to me evident," he says, " that an advantage would be gained by making the incandescent carbon filament as thin as possible, and my first experiments were directed to the attainment of this object by means of carbonized paper and carbonized cardboard."

He obtained, in 1848, from a paper merchant a great number of specimens of different kinds of paper and cardboard, and after cutting them into strips, and in several instances coiling them in spiral form, he packed them in a mass of powdered charcoal contained in a

---

[1] There is apparently an even earlier suggestion in a Belgian paper published in 1836, for using carbon, electrically heated *in vacuo*, as an illuminant for a miner's safety lamp.

fireclay crucible, which he then baked to a high temperature in a pottery kiln. In this way he obtained some beautifully thin and flexible strips and spirals of carbonized paper. Amongst the various means employed for producing and perfecting these carbon strips and spirals he adopted the method, well known in connection with the manufacture of carbon pencils for arc lamps and for Bunsen cells, of saturating the paper or card, and the carbon produced from it, with syrup, treacle, tar, and other liquids, which, on being heated, leave a large residue of carbon. These experiments extended over some years, and successful results, as regards the production of flexible and strong carbon spirals, had been arrived at by 1855 and probably earlier. In the course of these experiments he observed that the carbon resulting from the carbonization of parchmentized paper was exceptionally solid in texture and highly elastic and strong. If straight strips, they had sufficient pliancy to be bent into an arch ; and if let fall on a hard surface, they gave out quite a metallic note.

It should be remarked, in passing, that this carbonization of thin films or strips of carbonizable material was in itself technically new ; carbon in this form and condition of thinness and flexibility was previously unknown. It is also noteworthy that this mode of carbonization ultimately became the general mode of procedure in the carbonization of filaments for electric lamps.

The means employed for constructing a lamp for the purpose of these early experiments were characteristic in their simplicity and ready improvisation.

One form of lamp used at this time consisted simply of a glass bottle with a wide neck, closed with an indiarubber stopper ; the conducting wires passed through this stopper and held the carbon strip between their ends. Another form of lamp was improvised from a glass bell jar or shade inverted over a sole-plate like that of an air-pump. From these containers the air was exhausted as completely as possible by means of an ordinary air-pump with pistons and barrels. By means of a battery of 50 Callan cells he succeeded in rendering incandescent a carbon strip about ¼ inch broad, shaped in the form of an arch, 1½ inches high to the top of the arch. Sufficient battery power was not available to make the longer strips and spirals incandescent. Owing partly to there being some trace of air left within the glass container, and partly to the carbon becoming distorted under the action of unequal heating, it soon broke down.

This particular experiment was made in 1860, and though it ended in failure, so far as the production of a practical incandescent electric lamp was concerned, it had nevertheless established the fact that thin carbon conductors of almost any form and size and of a character suitable for producing light by incandescence could be produced by means of paper which had been buried in charcoal and carbonized by prolonged heating at a high temperature. It also indicated that at any rate one of the causes of failure was the impossibility of getting a sufficiently good vacuum with the means at that time available. It was clear that better results could not be obtained until some means were found for securing a better evacuation of the air.

But there was another all-important circumstance which impeded and discouraged further progress at this time. There was not in 1860 any practical way of getting a sufficiently cheap supply of electric current to make electric lighting, whether by the arc or by the incandescent lamp, a really practical proposition. The generation of electricity by means of voltaic cells, in spite of the improvements of Grove, Daniell, and others, was far too cumbrous and expensive to stand any chance of coming into general use for public or domestic lighting. Faraday's momentous discovery, in 1831, of the magneto-dynamic principle of generating electricity was still undeveloped. The production of electricity on this principle was not attempted on a large scale till 1849, and there was no permanent installation of electric lighting until 1862. In that year in Dungeness lighthouse the first commercial electric lighting plant was installed, consisting of a magneto-electric machine of a primitive type and a Serrin arc lamp.[1]

The next few years were destined to see an immense outburst of inventive activity in that branch of electrical engineering with which the names of Varley, Wheatstone, Siemens, Gramme, Brush, Wilde, Holmes, and many other foster-parents of the modern dynamo will always be associated.

Dynamo electric machines of various types were designed with ever-improving efficiency until in 1877 or thereabouts a point was reached when, at least for a particular class of lighting, *i.e.*, for lighthouses or the lighting of streets and great buildings, it could be demonstrated that electric lighting on that scale was not uneconomical; indeed, that it was actually more economical than gas-lighting on a similar scale.

During this period of electrical development Swan's experimental work was mainly devoted to photography and processes of photographic printing, and although the problem of the incandescent electric lamp still occupied his mind, no further advance was made towards its solution till 1877.

The invention of the mercury vacuum pump by Hermann Sprengel, in 1865, had shown the way to get a vacuum far superior to any previously attainable, and following upon this invention, Mr. Crookes (afterwards Sir William Crookes) had, in 1875, astonished the world by the exhibition of his radiometer and by the description of the improved means he employed for obtaining the near approach to a perfect vacuum which the construction of the radiometer demanded. It was the publication of Crookes' researches which led Swan to resume his

[1] Faraday witnessed the experimental lighting of the South Foreland lighthouse by electricity in 1856.

attempts to produce a satisfactory electric lamp by means of an incandescent carbon conductor in an evacuated glass container.

There was in Birkenhead at this time a young bank clerk, Charles H. Stearn by name, who, as Swan discovered through a chance advertisement concerning Crookes' radiometers, had been pursuing investigations which required high vacua, and who was familiar with all the manipulative refinements necessary for getting a very high degree of evacuation.

Swan, seeing the opportunity of testing the truth of the idea, firmly fixed in his mind, that strips of carbonized paper made incandescent in a very perfect vacuum would be indefinitely durable, wrote to Stearn asking if he would carry out the necessary experiments to establish this point. Stearn agreed to the proposal and at once commenced a series of experiments with carbon conductors of various forms and sizes, which Swan supplied, beginning with strips and spirals of carbonized paper and cardboard similar to those used in the abortive experiments of 1860. These were mounted in glass bulbs and exhausted to the highest possible degree by means of the Sprengel pump. Great difficulty was at first experienced in making firm contact between the ends of the carbon strip and the conducting wires between which it was held. To avoid these manipulative difficulties and to arrive more rapidly at a definite settlement of the vital question, namely, whether and under what conditions a carbon conductor could be made durable, the "film" (as the paper strip was then termed, for the name "filament" had not at that date been adopted) was for the time being discarded and other forms of carbon conductor were tried. Amongst the forms used were carbon wires, both straight and bent in an arch, and made of the same plastic material which is commonly used in manufacturing the thicker forms of carbon rod for electric arc lamps. These carbon wires were fitted in small platinum sockets, exactly as the thinner carbon filament of later days was mounted.

But other serious difficulties presented themselves in the early stages of these experiments and at first baffled every attempt to overcome them.

One trouble was the rapid wearing away and consequent breaking of the incandescent carbon ; another was the obscuration of the lamp bulb by a kind of black smoke. The uniform occurrence of these phenomena seemed to point irresistibly to the conclusion that the carbon of the filament was volatilized under the action of the enormous heat to which it was subjected. If, however, this idea of the volatilization of the carbon were founded in fact, any further attempt to render incandescent carbon lamps durable by means of a vacuum would be mere waste of time. Fortunately Swan did not accept as conclusive the experiments which seemed to show that the wasting of the filament and the blackening of the bulb were due to the volatility of carbon at the temperature employed. Further investigation showed that the better the evacuation, the less was the blackening of the glass. He held the view that the blackening occurred not by volatilization, but through the mechanical transport of the carbon particles, the residual air within the globe being the medium of their transport ; and he believed that if the air could be completely exhausted, this trouble would be overcome. Subsequent experience and research proved the soundness of both the diagnosis and the forecast.

But to get rid of this residuum of air was a formidable difficulty. It was found that, notwithstanding the lamp bulb had been very completely evacuated, the vacuum rapidly deteriorated owing to the evolution of air and other gases from the carbon, as soon as the current was turned on and the carbon began to incandesce. In order to meet this difficulty, the expedient was tried of first producing as nearly a perfect vacuum as could be got by exhausting the lamp bulb while the carbon was cold or only heated by a flame applied to the bulb from the outside, and then, when this point was reached, passing a strong current through the filament, so as to render it brilliantly incandescent, whilst the process of exhaustion was continued at this high temperature. By adopting this expedient it was found possible to obtain a vacuum that was not destroyed when the lamp was put into service. It was also found that the carbon in a lamp thus perfectly exhausted and sealed did not waste away, but was to all intents and purposes indefinitely durable. This important discovery, made before the close of 1878,[1] was in fact the key to the solution of the great problem of electric lighting by incandescence. It was indeed quite fundamental to success ; and the practice of continuing the exhaustion during the first incandescence of the lamp has ever since been an essential feature in commercial manufacture.

The knowledge gained by this discovery at once brought the manufacture of an incandescent lamp of reasonable durability within the range of practical achievement.

At a meeting of the Newcastle-upon-Tyne Chemical Society held on December 18th, 1878, Swan was able to show an incandescent carbon lamp, which consisted wholly of a glass bulb, pierced with two platinum wires, supporting between them a straight thin carbon conductor, $\frac{1}{25}$th inch in diameter. This lamp, after burning with a brilliant light for some minutes in his laboratory, had broken down solely owing to the current being excessive. On January 17th, 1879, the lecture was repeated and a similar lamp exhibited at Sunderland. The *Sunderland Echo* of January 18th, 1879, states : "The lecture was illustrated by an exhibition of the electric light, electric lamps, etc." It appears, therefore, that at this lecture a lamp was shown in actual operation.

The news that Swan had solved the problem of incandescent electric lighting by means of a vacuum lamp quickly spread through Newcastle, and he was invited to give a public lecture describing his invention. Accordingly, on February 3rd, 1879, he delivered a lecture on

[1] It was not, however, patented till 1880. See British Patent No. 8 of that year.

SWAN'S FIRST INCANDESCENT ELECTRIC LAMP
PUBLICLY SHOWN IN NEWCASTLE IN DECEMBER 1878

electric lighting to an audience of over 700 people in the lecture theatre of the Literary and Philosophical Society of Newcastle, Sir William Armstrong [1] presiding. At this lecture he exhibited in operation a lamp similar to that shown in the illustration opposite. The same lamp was exhibited again in operation at a lecture which he gave at the Town Hall in Gateshead on March 12th, 1879, before an audience of about 500.

But although the principles underlying the construction of a practical incandescent electric lamp had now been clearly established and several successful lamps had been made and exhibited, there was still experimental work to be done with a view to facilitating and improving the construction of the lamp ; and Swan continued, in co-operation with Stearn, to push on with these experiments, directing his efforts particularly to the improvement of the carbon conductor. As the straight carbon held between two fixed points showed a tendency to arch when incandescent, a hairpin form was tried and proved successful. But the most radical improvement was effected by the adoption and use of a *new* material instead of paper, thread, or other fibrous body as the carbon-forming substance. This material was cotton, converted by the action of sulphuric acid into a plastic and half-dissolved condition. By this treatment cotton yarn of an open texture (such as lamp cotton) becomes so agglutinated and compacted as entirely to lose its fibrous condition. It becomes transparent and, on drying, is hard like catgut, and can be scraped or planed down, by drawing through dies, to a wire of the most perfect roundness. It can, moreover, be bent into spirals and arches, and will retain its shape during carbonization. This material he called " parchmentized thread." This improvement was introduced early in 1880, and patented by him on November 27th of that year.[2] The carbon " filaments " (as by this time they had come to be called) made by

[1] Lord Armstrong (1st Baron), founder of the Elswick Manufacturing Works.   [2] Patent No. 4933.

E

this process had extraordinary strength and elasticity; they were also perfectly homogeneous, with the result that, when mounted in the lamps, they underwent little change, even under the action of an extremely high temperature.

The filaments so made were, for the purpose of mounting, formed with enlarged ends, held in tiny silver or copper sockets similar to that of a crayon-holder, and secured with a slip-ring. . But, later on, improved means were devised for making a good electrical contact between the carbon filament and the conducting wires. This was effected by a joint contrivance of Swan and Charles H. Gimingham, which consisted in tubulating the ends of the platinum wires and causing a deposit of carbon to take place at the point of junction of the filament and tube, so as to get a good electrical contact. This method of forming the carbon filament and of uniting it to the conducting wires remained the standard method of manufacturing incandescent electric lamps for several years.

Although he had produced and exhibited in December 1878 a lamp which he considered definitely proved the solution of the problem at which he had been working, Swan took no steps to patent the lamp as a whole. It was not until 1880 that he applied for and obtained his first patent in connection with the incandescent electric lamp. This patent was for the special process of evacuation, the essential feature of which was continuing the exhaustion of the bulb whilst the carbon was incandescent, for the purpose of removing all occluded gases. He also patented later the manufacture of carbon filaments from parchmentized thread, and the special means employed for attaching the filaments to the leading-in wires.

Swan held the opinion that the broad features of an incandescent lamp containing a carbon conductor in an evacuated glass globe were not patentable, having regard to the proposals which had been previously made for constructing a lamp having these main characteristics. In his view the only matters which were patentable at that date were those particular means and processes which made such a lamp practical.

Thomas Alva Edison, the young but already famous American inventor, apparently thought otherwise. Since the commencement of 1878 he had been attacking the problem of the subdivision of the electric light on lines similar to those on which Swan was at work. He realized that the right course was to have high resistance lamps adapted for giving a multiplicity of small units of light. Whilst Swan and Stearn were carrying on their joint experiments in Newcastle and Birkenhead, Edison was busily engaged in similar experiments in his well-equipped laboratory at Menlo Park, New Jersey, with several able assistants and a number of workmen, about a hundred people all told.[1]

From time to time rumours came across the Atlantic that Edison had attained or had nearly attained success. In October 1878 came the sensational announcement from Edison, "I have just solved the problem of the subdivision of the electric light indefinitely." This announcement was apparently made on the strength of an experiment with a high-resistance lamp, provided not with a carbon filament, but with a platinum wire spiral as the light-giving element; for Edison, being impressed at the outset with the seeming impossibility of using carbon, had turned his attention to platinum and alloys of platinum and iridium. English gas shares, which had slumped heavily on the publication of Edison's cable, recovered when it transpired that the announcement of success was somewhat premature. Scarcely any week passed, however, during this period without some further American Press proclamation of startling developments and successes in the laboratory at Menlo Park, until at last people in this country, at any rate, began to receive these reports with some measure of incredulity.

Here, for example, is an extract from *Nature*, December 25th, 1879:

[1] *History of the Electric Light*, Henry Schroeder.

" Once more the New York correspondent of the *Daily News* telegraphs of Mr. Edison's success in electric lighting. ' Mr. Edison,' we are told, ' has perfected an electric lamp of extraordinary simplicity with which he proposes a general illumination of the village of Menlo Park on New Year's Eve. He has discovered that a steady light is obtained by the incandescence of mere carbonized paper better than from any other known substance.' "

This and similar announcements appearing in other papers evoked from Swan the following letter, which was published in *Nature*, January 1st, 1880:

" I observe in *Nature*, vol xxi. p. 187, a statement to the effect that Mr. Edison has adopted the use of carbon in his new electric lamp and that the carbon he uses is charred paper or card in the shape of a horseshoe. Fifteen years ago I used charred paper and card in the construction of an electric lamp on the incandescent principle. I used it too in the shape of a horseshoe, precisely as you say Mr. Edison is now using it. I did not then succeed in obtaining the durability which I was in search of, but I have since made many experiments on the subject, and within the last six months [1] I have, I believe, completely conquered the difficulty which led to previous failure, and I am now able to produce a perfectly durable electric lamp by means of incandescent carbon.—*Underhill, Low Fell, December 29th,* 1879."

As Edison was from time to time applying for British patents in connection with the incandescent electric lamp, Stearn was keenly apprehensive of the risk of his collaborator being anticipated by Edison obtaining priority

---

[1] He had already established the practicability of a vacuum lamp with carbon conductor twelve months ago, but not with the horseshoe form of filament, which he considered the best form for practical purposes. The experiments here referred to eventuated early in 1880 in the production of a filament from parchmentized cotton thread. This filament made the manufacture of the lamps commercial.

of patent right; and, after the success achieved in December 1878, he repeatedly urged Swan to protect his invention by patent.

Swan, however, influenced by the reason above mentioned, and relying on his already published achievement, made no haste to patent his invention. This was probably a tactical error. Stearn's apprehensions proved well founded. On November 10th, 1879, Edison applied for and obtained a British patent, covering, in the broadest terms, the invention of an incandescent electric lamp possessing as its cardinal features a carbon filament within a glass receiver from which the air had been exhausted.[1]

At this date it appears that Edison had reverted to carbon as the light-giving element, and that this patent specification was the outcome of an experiment which he had made on October 21st, 1879, with a lamp containing a loop of carbonized sewing thread mounted in an evacuated bulb.[2] This form of filament, however, was later found to be impracticable for commercial use, and Edison thereupon resorted to carbonized paper. Hence the reference to lamps made with carbonized paper in the passage from *Nature* quoted above.

Early in 1880 Edison discontinued the use of carbonized paper and adopted carbonized strips of bamboo.

So far as the practical manufacture of lamps by Edison is concerned, there appears to be no record of any exhibition of Edison lamps in this country prior to 1880. The earliest Edison lamps seen in England were, it is believed, six lamps brought over by Mr. Johnson, who was Edison's commercial agent. These lamps were on view in Queen Victoria Street in February 1880. Edison's lamps were exhibited at the Paris Exhibition, September 1881, and at the Crystal Palace in the autumn of 1882. The filaments in those early Edison lamps were made from bamboo fibre in accordance with the process described in

---

[1] British Patent No. 4576.
[2] *History of Electric Light*, Henry Schroeder, p. 48.

his patent of 1880, and not in accordance with the process described in his original carbon filament lamp patent of 1879. It is to be observed, therefore, that for more than a year after Swan had invented and adopted parchment-ized thread as the filament material, Edison was still using bamboo. But it was the parchmentized thread and not the bamboo which survived and became the universally used basis of the filament, and so continued until it was superseded some five or six years later by the squirted filament, also the invention of Swan.

By the summer of 1880 lamps made with parch-mentized cotton filaments had reached a degree of uniformity and durability which satisfied Swan that their manufacture on an industrial scale was now a practical proposition.

Amongst those whose advice he sought at this juncture was a young electrical engineer, R. E. Crompton,[1] who had already at that date made a name as the inventor and manufacturer of electric arc lamps, and whose continued practical contributions to the advancement of electrical engineering during the past fifty years have kept him in a position of well-deserved distinction in the forefront of electrical progress. Crompton and Swan had not actually met up to that time, but Swan had already purchased some of Crompton's arc lamps and had corresponded with him on the subject of electrical distribution. Colonel Crompton has kindly furnished the following descrip-tion of his first meeting with Swan in the autumn of 1880.

"A gentleman (Mr. Morgan I think his name was) whom I believed to be one of the travellers of Messrs. Mawson & Swan, sent in his card to my office, 4, Queen Victoria Street, and said he had come with a request of such an urgent nature that I must take it as a mandate that I would accompany him that very evening to Newcastle to see Mr. Swan. I was not allowed to go home to get any clothes or sleeping things, but was carried off to New-

---

[1] Now Colonel R. E. Crompton, C.B.

castle, and was there and then taken to Mr. Swan's laboratory, introduced to him, and shown a row of sealed glass bulbs containing carbon filaments which he informed me had been pumped by a form of Sprengel pump, invented by Mr. C. H. Stearn, to a higher degree of vacuum than had hitherto been considered practically obtainable. The filaments, he explained, were mounted on platinum terminals and were formed of cotton which had been made into cellulose before carbonizing.

"After explaining this, he had a gas-engine driving a Gramme machine started up, and lamps were switched on and glowed in a most satisfactory manner. He asked my opinion as to what could be done with it, and told me he was shortly afterwards to lecture to the Philosophical Society at Newcastle, and begged that I would be present to take part in the discussion, as he considered that I, as an apostle of the arc lamp, was to some extent in rivalry with him. He wished me to understand that there was a distinct place for the two kinds of illumination.

"This was the first time I came in contact with him, and I was then struck with the extreme fairness and openness of his mind, and with his extraordinary modesty."

When the first Swan Electric Lamp Company was formed in Newcastle, Crompton was appointed Chief Engineer, and he played an important part and rendered valuable assistance to Swan in the negotiations which shortly afterwards led to the formation of the larger London company.

The lecture to which Colonel Crompton alludes was one on " Electric Lighting," which Swan delivered on October 20th, 1880, in the lecture room of the Literary and Philosophical Society of Newcastle, Sir William Armstrong being in the chair. At the conclusion of his address he gave the signal for the seventy gas jets which lighted the room to be turned out, and then (with a suddenness which in those days seemed quite magical) transformed darkness into light by switching on twenty of his own lamps, producing an illumination which, as compared with gas light, had a very brilliant effect. The occasion was of historic interest, for it was the first time, at any rate in Europe, that the interior of any public building had been lighted by incandescent electric lamps.

In the following month (on November 24th) a similarly striking and successful demonstration was given to the Society of Telegraph Engineers, as the body of electricians which has since become the " Institution of Electrical Engineers " was then called.

Amongst those who took part in the discussion upon that occasion one notes the names of John Hopkinson, Alexander Siemens, Tyndall, Ayrton, Latimer Clark, Crompton, and Fletcher Moulton (afterwards Lord Moulton). Though there appears to have been a general agreement that there was scope for this infant alongside its well-established elder brother, the arc lamp, there seems to have been no prophetic inkling in the minds of any of the speakers as to the brilliant future that lay before these simple little bulbs, or as to the immensely important part that they were destined to play in the development of electrical industry.

Nevertheless, the public interest that these demonstrations aroused, both amongst men of science and men of business, was considerable. Electrical engineers and contractors hurried to Newcastle to see the lamp, and to discuss schemes for its exploitation.

Amongst electricians with whom Swan thus came into contact mention should be made in particular of Henry Edmunds,[1] then a young and enterprising electrical engineer, who had already had experience in the exploitation of electrical inventions in America and elsewhere, and who now offered his services, which were accepted, and proved most valuable in introducing Swan's lamp to the public.

---

[1] See *Reminiscences of a Pioneer*, by Henry Edmunds, M.I.E.E.

THE FIRST COMMERCIAL SWAN LAMP MADE BY THE SWAN ELECTRIC LAMP COMPANY
AT SOUTH BENWELL, NEWCASTLE IN 1881

(From a photograph taken and presented by the Science Museum of South Kensington.)

But, before exploitation could proceed, arrangements had to be made for the manufacture of the lamp on a commercial scale.

A small company was accordingly formed in Newcastle, called " The Swan Electric Lamp Company, Ltd.," and a factory was started at Benwell, just outside Newcastle, for the manufacture of the lamp, which had hitherto been made partly at Low Fell, where the filament was formed and carbonized, and partly at Stearn's workshop in Birkenhead, where the glass-blowing, mounting of the filament, and the evacuation and sealing of the bulb had been carried out. No glass-blowers expert enough for the highly skilled work required for the lamp manufacture could be found in England, other than the young glass-blower, Fred Topham,[1] whom Stearn had employed. German glass-blowers from the Thuringian district were, therefore, imported and Topham was brought over from Birkenhead to instruct them. The delicate work of forming the filament ready for carbonization, which work had in the early lamps been done by the ladies of the inventor's own household, was given to a staff of specially trained girls.

In the organization of the lamp manufacture on an industrial scale, in the design of subsidiary features of the lamp, and in its adaptation for the various special purposes for which its use rapidly became apparent, Swan was greatly assisted by Stearn and Charles Gimingham. He was also helped by his brother Alfred, who devoted himself more especially to devising suitable means of attaching the lamp to its holder, and who, later on, by the introduction of " vitrite " as the insulating material for use in the base or cap, made an important contribution to the improvement of this part of the lamp.

Thus came about the complete fulfilment of the idea which Swan had first conceived in 1845, and had nursed and cherished for thirty years, until in the " hatch of

---

[1] Later the inventor of the " Topham spinning box " and other ingenious devices used in the manufacture of artificial silk.

time," thanks to the invention of Hermann Sprengel and the skilful assistance of Charles Stearn, he was able ultimately, by a short period of intensive research and experiment, to bring it to fruition.

And thus, through Swan's invention, there was established in this country by the beginning of 1881 the first commercial manufacture of the incandescent electric lamp. It was an event fraught with far-reaching consequences; for from that small beginning sprang not only a vast industry of lamp manufacture, but also, indirectly, the immense crop of industries which we now see engaged in the production of electrical equipment—for which up to that date the demand had been small or non-existent—such as generating plant and machinery, electric cable and wire, insulating material, electrical measuring instruments, electrical fittings, and the other multifarious apparatus nowadays accessory to the use of the incandescent electric lamp.

CHAPTER VI

THE first private residence, after the inventor's own, to be lighted by the new incandescent lamps was the house of his friend, Sir William Armstrong, at Cragside, near Rothbury. Swan personally supervised the installation there in December 1880. It was also the first hydro-electric generating plant in the country, the motive power being obtained from a waterfall in the grounds. There was also an experimental lighting of part of Aln-wick Castle about the same time. Amongst other early private installations should be mentioned the lighting of the house of Sir William Spottiswoode, President of the Royal Society, and the lighting of the Scottish home of Sir William Thomson (afterwards Lord Kelvin), who had from the first evinced a very keen and friendly interest in Swan's invention, and had consented to act as honorary consultant to the new company. His house was lighted with the new lamp from cellar to attic early in 1881.

Apart from the early displays on the premises of Messrs. Mawson & Swan in Mosley Street, James Coxon, an enterprising linen-draper of Newcastle, was the first to adopt the Swan lamp for shop-lighting, thus proving himself a pioneer in what has been one of the most extensively exploited applications of the incandescent electric lamp, namely, its use for purposes of advertisment.

The fashion for the new means of lighting spread with amazing rapidity. Its applicability for marine use was quickly perceived by shipping companies. The pioneers in this direction were the "Inman Line," whose ship, the *City of Richmond*, was the first British vessel to be lighted by incandescent lamps. She was fitted out in June 1881.

The manner in which the Swan lamp came to be introduced into the Navy is told by Henry Edmunds in his

Reminiscences.[1] It appears that early in 1881 Captain J. A. Fisher, R.N. (afterwards Admiral Lord Fisher of Kilverstone) was dining with Sir William Spottiswoode, and was much struck by seeing the dinner-table illuminated by six or eight incandescent lamps supplied to him by Swan. Captain Fisher was so much interested in this mode of lighting that he wrote to Swan asking whether it would be possible to have the lamps introduced into the Royal Navy for his new ship, the *Inflexible.* The answer was in the affirmative, and Mr. Edmunds was asked to proceed at once to Portsmouth to demonstrate the suitability of the lamps on the spot.

The rest of the narrative can best be given in Mr. Edmunds' own words :—

" At Portsmouth I was met by Captain Fisher, who took me over the *Inflexible,* and invited me to lunch at his club ; he had arranged for a demonstration in a shed in the dockyard, which had been darkened for the purpose. It had two parallel bare copper wires suspended by strings from the ceiling, passing outside to a search-light-dynamo driven by a semi-portable engine, controlled by signals between two bo'suns, one inside the shed and the other outside. The seamen communicated by whistle, and the speed of the engine was carefully adjusted so that the incandescent lamps ran brightly without being distressed. At that period we had no fuses, no volt-meters, no ampère-meters, and practically no switches ; and it required no little care to get proper adjustment.

" At last we got our lamps to glow satisfactorily, and at that moment the Admiral was announced. Captain Fisher had warned me that I must be careful how I answered any question, for the Admiral was of the stern old school, and prejudiced against all new-fangled notions. The Admiral appeared, resplendent in gold lace, and accompanied by such a bevy of ladies that I was strongly reminded of the character in *H.M.S. Pinafore,* with his sisters, and his cousins and his aunts. The Admiral

---

[1] *Reminiscences of a Pioneer,* by Henry Edmunds.

immediately asked if I had seen the *Inflexible.* I replied that I had. 'Have you seen the powder magazine ? ' 'Yes! I have been to it.' 'What would happen to one of these little glass bubbles in the event of a broadside ? ' I did not think it would affect them. 'How do you know ? You've never been in a ship during a broadside ! ' I saw Captain Fisher's eye fixed upon me, and a sailor was dispatched for some gun-cotton.

" Evidently everything had been already prepared, for he quickly returned with a small tea-tray about two feet long, upon which was a layer of gun-cotton, powdered over with black gunpowder. The Admiral asked if I was prepared to break one of the lamps over the tray. I replied that I could do so quite safely ; for the glowing lamp would be cooled down by the time it fell amongst the gun-cotton. I took a cold chisel, smashed a lamp and let it fall. The company saw the light extinguished and a few pieces of glass fall on the tray. There was no flash, and the gunpowder and gun-cotton remained as before. There was a short pause, while the Admiral gazed on the tray. Then he turned and said to Captain Fisher, ' We'll have this light in the *Inflexible.*' " [1]

About the same time the light was also installed in many public buildings. In June 1881 a trial installation with Swan lamps was fitted up in the House of Commons, and gave great satisfaction. In October 1881, on the Brighton line, a special train was run from Victoria to Brighton and back, with a saloon lighted with Swan lamps, the current being supplied by Faure [2] storage batteries.

In 1882 the Mansion House, the British Museum, the Royal Academy, and many other large buildings were illuminated with Swan lamps. The first theatre to adopt the new lamp was the Savoy. There, through the enter-

---

[1] *Reminiscences of a Pioneer*, Henry Edmunds.

[2] Camille Faure, a French electrician, who made important improvements in the voltaic cell invented by M. Gaston Planté.

prise of D'Oyley Carte, its famous manager, the incandescent lamp made its début with a truly spectacular display. The stage was lit by 824 lamps, and there were 370 more in other parts of the house. Later on, in a performance of *Iolanthe*, a further very effective use was made of the incandescent lamp as part of the adornment of the performers themselves. The Fairy Queen waved a wand tipped with a glow lamp that went in and out at will and the chorus of fairies with tiny lamps twinkling in their hair " glittered like a swarm of fireflies."

It should not be forgotten that in these primitive days the difficulty of providing an installation for a private house or a public building was very considerable. Each installation required its own generating plant, its gas or steam engine, its dynamo, and in most cases its set of storage cells. Then, again, the systems and methods of wiring were, to say the least of it, somewhat empirical and precarious, and the fittings, such as switches and attachments for hanging or holding the lamps, were all of a most primitive and makeshift description.

In all of these early installations Swan took a personal interest, in many cases supervising and inspecting the work as it progressed, and advising on points of doubt or difficulty that arose. But innumerable other calls and distractions crowded in upon him. There were invitations to deliver lectures in all parts of the country; there were interested strangers who desired to see the lamp and discuss its potentialities with the inventor (and no one who sought out Swan for information or advice, however inopportune and tiresome the visit might be, was ever rebuffed or treated with anything but the utmost courtesy); there were pressing questions arising in connection with the newly formed company and suggestions for its merger into a larger London company; there were, above all, ideas ever thronging through his mind for the further improvement and new applications of his lamp and for the improvement of the electrical apparatus that was required in connection with it.

In the midst of all these preoccupations came one distraction which, though somewhat in the nature of a " busman's holiday," was, at any rate, as close an approximation to a genuine holiday as Swan permitted himself at this busy time. The Paris Exhibition, held in the Palais de l'Industrie in the Champs Elysées in the latter part of 1881, gave the first great opportunity for a comprehensive display of the electric light. It was in fact a show, as the *Times* correspondent says, " greater than anything that has ever been seen in the world." All the competing systems of illumination by arc-lamp and incandescent lamp were represented there ; a galaxy of rival constellations, lighting the different parts of the Exhibition buildings, the former with dazzling but intermittent brilliance; the latter with a softer and steadier radiance.

The Swan Electric Light Company had organized an exhibit of its lamps there under the supervision of Henry Edmunds, and—" proximus ardet Ucalegon "—Edison's lamps were all aglow in a neighbouring stand. Hiram Maxim and Lane-Fox were other exhibitors of incandescent electric lamps. The Salle des Séances was also lit by Swan lamps. This was the famous hall where the international representatives met in congress and settled for general future use the value of the fundamental electrical units, coining the words " ampère," " coulomb," and " farad," to rank with " volt " and " ohm " as recognized standards of electrical measurement.

Though the effect of all this illumination was very splendid, it was achieved at no little risk. There were no protecting devices in those days such as fuses and cut-outs ; and the insulation of the wiring and cables was not above suspicion. The danger of fire through a short-circuit or faulty connection was therefore considerable, and in fact a fire did break out in the French section, but it was soon suppressed. Swan was keenly alive to this risk, and had additional safeguards introduced at every point of possible danger.

Besides the exhibits of electric lighting there was a vast array of other exhibits illustrating the most recent developments in kindred fields of electrical industry. In the telegraphy and telephony section Swan heard for the first time the music of the opera transmitted by telephone. "Last night," he writes, "I had a great treat. I heard the opera, the Grand Opera, but I was not in the Opera House, only in the telephone rooms here. I heard them no less than five different times for a minute or two each time. I heard soprano, bass, tenor, singing and orchestral music with a clearness and purity of sound that was perfectly miraculous and more than a mile away!" In the section devoted to apparatus for generating and storing electricity, he saw Faure's adaptation of the Planté secondary cell or storage battery, and his thoughts were turned to a scheme, which for some months past had occupied his mind, for improving this type of storage battery.

Other incidents and impressions of his visit appear from the following extracts from his letters:

Swan Eclairage Electrique Incandescent,
September 23rd, 1881.

"I am taking the opportunity of a spare and quiet moment to tell you of our continued success.

"Last night in the Salle du Congrès there was a meeting of the Society of Telegraph Engineers. We, of course, lighted the hall with our lamps. There was only one opinion as to the manner in which it was done. We turned the lights in and out to accommodate the lecturer, who had magic-lantern demonstrations, and this was done quite as promptly as if gas, instead of electricity, had been the lighting agent. I am going to spend a part of the evening at the house of M. Planté, the inventor of the secondary battery of which the Faure battery is only a development. I anticipate a great treat, for M. Planté has called upon me here and I already know from this visit and from what the Count du Moncel told me of him that he is an extremely interesting man.

"Did I tell you that it was settled that we were to light the interior of the Grand Opera House? Edison, Lane-Fox, and others are to light parts of the buildings also. I do not know which of us has the best part, for there are splendid opportunities for effective lighting in several of the rooms and staircases besides that which we have in the Opera itself."

PARIS,
September 24th, 1881.

"Everything at the Exhibition has so far gone very favourably for us. Everyone is complimentary in the extreme. Certainly our rooms look well. The buffet is exquisite so far as our light is concerned. I spent a pleasant evening at the house of M. Planté. His house is a study and a laboratory—all devoted to his work. I think he is a bachelor! *All the tables* are crowded with apparatus and the only unoccupied furniture are chairs. I question whether M. Planté has a bed—at all events he told me that he did not sleep, and that gives a certain ground for the presumption. He is a perfect gentleman, Spanish in his politeness ; ' his house was mine.' He has presented me with a copy of each of his works, which are very scarce and very interesting."

October 21st, 1881.

"I was fondly hoping it would not be necessary to write again from here, for that I should have the delight of seeing you before a letter could reach you—but I find myself still here instead of on my way to London. The announcement was at last definitely made that the awards would be made to-day, and I am only just returned from the ceremony. It was at the Conservatoire of Music, under the presidency of one of the Ministers—the jury and commissioners all being present and a magnificent choir of singers. After a fine musical performance on

F

the part of the choir, the President made a speech, then the Chief Commissioner, then the Secretary read his report and the names of those who had received awards. First, Diplomas of Honour, Edison being of that class. Then another kind of diploma. Then Gold Medal awards; then Silver Medals. I was in the Gold Medal class. The jury had a difficult task to perform and I suppose did the best they could with it.

"The patent business is all in a perfectly unsettled state. There are no new enquiries from likely buyers of the patent for France,[1] but plenty of enquiries for lamps, and the most serious question is waiting to be debated, namely, whether in face of the demand for lamps we should begin lamp-making in France. We are asked to make an offer for lighting the Grand Opera for three years."

At the conclusion of the Exhibition, Swan received the decoration of the Legion of Honour in recognition of his inventions.

On his return to England, towards the end of October, he was again deeply absorbed in the vortex of business and experiment.

The establishment of a lamp factory in France having been decided upon, he looked round for some one competent to superintend this undertaking. It was not easy to find anyone suitable for the job; for electrical engineers did not exist in those days. Again, however, fortune favoured him in his choice. A young mechanical engineer, James Swinburne[2] by name, was introduced to him, and Swan, perceiving him to be a man of parts, asked him to undertake it. So Swinburne was given three weeks' intensive training as an electrician at the lamp factory at Newcastle and was then sent out to set up a similar factory in Paris.

He was commissioned to call at Antwerp on the way

---

[1] £40,000 had been offered, but this offer was refused by the agents.

[2] Now a Fellow of the Royal Society and eminent as an electrician, consulting engineer, and expert witness.

to make a lamp there in order to comply with the Belgian patent law requirements. It took three weeks to make that lamp under the conditions then obtaining. A bit of a saw-mill, boarded off, served as the works. The plant was a Gramme (series wound) dynamo whose speed varied from about 500 to 1500 revolutions from minute to minute. The lamp was finally completed. It cost about £100 and was sold at quite another price to the owner of the sawmill, with a caution that he should above all things avoid running it.

The factory at Paris was got going after surmounting the same sort of difficulties that beset the commercial manufacture of lamps in Newcastle, *e.g.*, glass-blowers had to be imported from Germany, as French workmen could not work soda glass. By the end of 1881, however, France was being supplied with French-made Swan lamps.

In 1882 Swan sold his American patents to the Brush Company of Cleveland, U.S.A., and Swinburne went out to assist in starting the manufacture of the Swan lamp there. The intention of the Brush Company was to carry on the lamp manufacture in conjunction with the manufacture of the Brush secondary battery which they were then endeavouring to perfect. This battery, however, never became a commercial success, and the manufacture of Swan lamps in America died down.

Amongst the various applications of his lamp which engaged Swan's attention at this time was one which would perhaps naturally be uppermost in the mind of a Tynesider, namely, its use as a miner's safety lamp.

The first embodiment of his idea in this regard consisted of a strong glass bell, defended by a cage of wires enclosing a small incandescent lamp. The lamp was connected by a flexible conductor directly with the main source of supply at the head of the shaft, or with an intermediate electrical reservoir in the shape of a portable case of storage cells that could be carried on a trolley or by other suitable means to the spot where the miner was working. An arrangement of this type was shown at a meeting of the scientific societies of Liverpool in 1881, and a few months later at a meeting of the Mining Institute of Newcastle.

But he saw that a lamp of this kind did not meet all the requirements of the case, and he set to work, therefore, to devise a portable safety lamp which, with equal weight, would give a better light and more absolute immunity from danger of explosion than was afforded by the " Davy," the " Clanny," the " Geordy," and other similar types of lamp generally used in the pits at that time.

As the outcome of experiments extending over a period of five years, he succeeded in designing a miner's portable electric safety lamp which, for a weight comparable to that of an ordinary miner's lamp, gave a light averaging two candles over a period of ten hours. This was two or three times as much as the best safety lamp gave at that date. One of the features of this lamp was a secondary cell of ingenious design, in which a fibrous form of lead was employed which held the sulphuric acid like a sponge, and so prevented its spilling if the battery was tilted. It was also provided with a fire-damp indicator, a spiral of platinum wire enclosed in a tube to which outside air could be admitted. If fire-damp was present, the platinum spiral glowed with abnormal brightness when current passed. The indicator also included a device for measuring the percentage of fire-damp present.

Though in every respect a thoroughly practical and successful design, the cost of the lamp militated against its adoption. It is only in comparatively recent years, thanks to cheapened means of manufacture and a simplification of construction due to many ingenious designers who have since turned their attention to this problem, that portable electric safety lamps have come into practical use in coal mines ; but even now, owing to their weight and cost, their use is limited.

A specimen of Swan's portable miner's lamp is now to be seen in the electrical section of the Science Museum at South Kensington.

Another matter which engaged his attention on his return from Paris was the improvement of Planté's storage battery.

In October 1879 Swan had devised and exhibited a modification of Planté's battery, merely differing from it in form, having the lead surface enormously extended by the use of frills of lead foil. Later he took the further step of depositing, by electrolytic action, spongy lead in the interstices of the frills.

The idea of using spongy lead in this manner in some measure anticipated the development of the Planté cell by Faure and de Méritens, specimens of whose inventions Swan had carefully examined at the Paris Exhibition. But these improvements still left the storage battery a very cumbrous and imperfect piece of apparatus, and Swan had, even before the Paris Exhibition, applied for provisional protection for an improvement on the Faure battery, which he now set about perfecting. In the Faure battery as commonly used at that date, a cloth wrapping was employed to hold the oxide and spongy lead in contact with the surface of the plate. Instead of this somewhat clumsy arrangement, Swan proposed and designed a cellular lead plate, into the cells of which the spongy lead could be neatly packed so as to expose a large surface of active material. By this means the storage capacity of the cell for a given weight was very greatly increased. This invention was patented in 1881,[1] and the manufacture of cells on this principle was taken up by the Electric Power and Storage Company, and gave practicality to the employment of secondary batteries on a large scale. The idea embodied in Swan's cellular plate, though slightly modified in various ways, has remained the central principle of all improvements in secondary batteries since Planté made his great

[1] No. 2272.

discovery, and has proved a valuable contribution to the means of storing electricity and maintaining constant pressure at the generating station.

The early part of 1882 found the Swan family at Lancing, in a house lent to them by a friend, but Swan could only be there at intervals between his business and lecturing engagements.

As a lecturer he was much in demand, and a large amount of his time was occupied in lecturing in various parts of the country to societies, learned and unlearned, on electricity and its uses, and in particular upon his invention of the incandescent electric lamp, his miner's lamp, and his improvements in connection with electric storage batteries.

If much of his time was taken in delivering these lectures, still more was spent in composing them. It was not that he was slow in putting his ideas upon paper; indeed he wrote with considerable rapidity and facility from a mind brimming over with abundance of matter. But he was extremely fastidious as to the ultimate form in which to present his ideas to the public. Lectures would be written and rewritten many times before a draft was reached that satisfied him as to its composition and phrasing. In this work of recasting and fair-copying his lectures his wife was of great assistance to him—as is testified by the innumerable drafts and fair copies that remain in her clear, neat manuscript.

Amongst the more important of his lectures delivered at this date were those given to the Literary and Philosophical Society at Newcastle (with Sir William Armstrong in the chair) and to the Royal Institution in London (one of the Friday evening lectures) on the "Storage of Electricity"; to the Northern Institute of Mining and Mechanical Engineers on the "Miner's Safety Lamp"; and to the Society of Telegraph Engineers (which was later renamed the "Institution of Electrical Engineers") on "Electric Lighting by Incandescence," Sir Frederick Bramwell being in the chair.

JOSEPH WILSON SWAN AT THE AGE OF 54

A lecture was also given at the Crystal Palace, where an Electrical Exhibition was opened in March 1882.

Besides this lecturing and his continual experimental work he had an immense amount of business to attend to, and this year was one of terrific wear and tear. In the north the lamp factory at Benwell and the dry-plate works at Low Fell, as well as the older businesses, constantly required his oversight and direction. The manufacture of lamps recently started in Paris, and later removed to Lille, called for attention. The sale of the foreign patents involved much troublesome negotiation. The reconstruction of the company which had been formed in Newcastle, and which now was expanded into a larger concern under the title "The Swan United Electric Lighting Company Ltd.," was another transaction which absorbed a good deal of his time. The formation of this new company occasioned Swan a good deal of worry, but further trouble was in store. No sooner was the formation of the new company successfully accomplished than the Edison Company, which had recently been floated to acquire and exploit Edison's electric lamp patents, commenced proceedings against the Swan Company for infringement of these patents.

There was also at this time another matter which gave Swan great concern. Important legislation was in course of progress through Parliament, designed to regulate the future development of electric lighting. This Bill gave rise to much discussion and controversy amongst electricians. Swan was particularly anxious that nothing should be done in the way of regulative control which would unduly hamper the growth and extended use of electricity for lighting. In this, however, he was doomed to disappointment, for the Bill, as passed into law,[1] proved a serious hindrance and discouragement to electrical enterprise in this country, with the result that in England the growth and development of electric lighting and kindred uses of electricity lagged far behind the rapid strides made

[1] Electric Lighting Act, 1882.

in other countries such as America, France, Germany, and Switzerland. With all this press of business to attend to it is no wonder that Swan found his hands full. A board meeting of the new company, followed by a scientific discussion with Sir William Thomson over luncheon ; an appointment at his patent agent's office to settle a patent specification; a visit to the committee rooms of the House of Commons with Dr. Merz or Mr. Spence Watson; a ceremonial dinner at the Crystal Palace, or a conversazione of one of the learned societies, and then up next morning about 5 a.m. to catch a train back to Newcastle to attend to other pressing business—such would fairly represent one of Swan's days at this time. His letters to his wife naturally reflect the stress and strain of this harassing period.

GREAT NORTHERN HOTEL,
May 11*th*, 1882.

" To-day has been a repetition of yesterday so far as unremitting occupation goes, and it is only now that I have a moment in which to breathe freely. It was expected and fully arranged that the agreement for the carrying out of the reconstruction and enlargement of our company would be signed to-day, but difficulties have arisen and these have caused delay, and it is still a question whether or not they will be got over. I am neither eager nor anxious about the change, for if in one way it may be an advantage, in another way—in the matter of responsibility and labour—it will load me still more heavily and *much* more heavily."

THE OFFICES OF MESSRS. CROMPTON & CO., LTD.,
MANSION HOUSE BUILDINGS,
June 22*nd*, 1882.

" I'm afraid that you will think that I have forgotten that I have an anxious and sympathetic wife, only to be reached for the time being by letter or telegram, and who is not reached by either of these admirable and commodious means of communication. But in fact I have not merely been busy—that says far too little and misrepresents the actual case—my thoughts have all been pre-occupied to the extent that I have been almost paralysed in matters of pressing action; even a telegram has remained for a time unread, or if read and requiring an answer—unanswered. It is simply that business has been very pressing, and nothing more serious than that."

Messrs. Crompton & Co., Ltd.,
Anchor Iron Works, Chelmsford,
July 31*st,* 1882.

" While I am waiting for Mr. Crompton to go back with me to London, I take the opportunity of reporting the day's proceedings so far.

" I had a long committee this morning, and after it there were so many things to be discussed between Mr. Crompton and myself that I travelled down here for the sake of saving his time, and to see the works. They are very much extended since I was here about six months ago, and they have the look of being under good management and capable of doing a large quantity of good work.

" Mr. Stearn is here from Paris about extensions of the factory there. I am to meet him at the hotel when I get back.

" Yesterday afternoon I went to Mr. Moulton's,[1] and had a conversation with him as to the ' action.' He would very much like to help us, but fears, unless we make some very strong effort, he will have to go against us. There is a letter from Sir Wm. Thomson to our attorney. He will give evidence in our favour. It is very good of him ! No doubt he would rather keep out of it if only he consulted his own feeling and convenience."

Swan United Electric Lighting Co., Ltd.,
Coleman Street,
August 1882.

" As I may be called off at any moment to attend to this bothering legal business, I will snatch the present for a few lines to you.

[1] J. Fletcher Moulton, Q.C., afterwards Lord Moulton.

" I need not say how glad I was to receive your telegram telling me that the lamp I used at the lecture is in safety and unbroken.[1]

" I have made an affidavit denying the contention of the Edison Company, and it is expected that to-day the question will be decided whether they obtain an injunction to restrain our Company from making lamps. I do not think there is the slightest doubt the application for an injunction will be refused; our opponents will, therefore, gain no advantage of any kind at this stage of the proceedings."

The application for an interlocutory injunction was refused; and, thanks to wiser counsels prevailing, overtures were made for a peaceful settlement of the action. These speedily resulted in an amalgamation of the two rival companies under the somewhat lengthy title of "The Edison & Swan United Electric Light Company, Ltd."

The British Association, meeting at Southampton towards the end of August of that year, afforded a pleasant interlude from business.

The British Association Reception Rooms,
Southampton,
August 25*th,* 1882.

To H. S.

" I am here, you see. I arrived last night, and was soon housed very comfortably at the S.W. Hotel. After dinner I went with Sir Wm. Armstrong to a corner of the Hartley Rooms, where there was a concord of sweet sounds and concourse of most of the great people of science. I saw Sir Wm. Thomson and a great many persons I knew. I breakfasted with Sir Wm. Thomson this morning and walked with him to his ' section.' I have been at Section A all day, and have listened to several interesting papers, but came away vexed with

---

[1] The lamp used at the lecture to the Literary and Philosophical Society of Newcastle on February 3rd, 1879, and relied on by the Swan Company as an anticipation of Edison's patent.

a sense of partial failure in criticizing a paper by Mr. Sprague. I spoke too long and too loosely, that is with no particular point. . . ."

August 26th, 1882.

" I went to a lecture by Sir Wm. Thomson on Tides. He was, as usual, lucid—even in dealing with such an abstruse subject—amusing and enthusiastic. He is a charming lecturer, though full of oddities."

Besides providing intellectual entertainment, the British Association, then as now, made arrangements for members to visit places of interest in the surrounding neighbourhood.

S.W. HOTEL, SOUTHAMPTON,
August 27th, 1882.

To H. S.

" Why did you not come with me! Here I am all alone—wondering what I shall do, and sorely wanting you to help me to find what I shall do to make the most of my half-holiday here! I know your being here to enjoy it with me would in every case double my pleasure. I was wanting you so very much yesterday when we went to Broadlands.[1] I had not before seen the beautiful country about here till then. We drove to Broadlands, eight miles, with ever-increasing charm of country about us till we reached Romsey, an old village close to Broadlands. There we saw, alone at first, but at last in company with a crowd of tourists, the Abbey. The Rector gave in very good style an historical account of it, which much added to the interest it arouses. Then we went to Broadlands."

SALISBURY PLAIN. ON ONE OF THE TUMULI FRONTING
STONEHENGE AND IN SIGHT OF IT,
3.15 *p.m., August 27th,* 1882.

" I stopped in writing this morning to go by train to Salisbury. I longed for the quiet and wide expanse of view which I knew I would obtain here, and so I arranged

[1] Lord Mount Temple's country seat.

to come and spend the day here, and here I am, close to Stonehenge, but like the distance better, partly because there are some beer-drinking and rowdy young fellows about the Stones just now; they will be gone presently no doubt, because their beer will be gone. I saw the great stone bottle nearly empty.

" The quiet is delightful and the solitude is delightful too, with nothing outward but the wind and flowers for company. I am quite alone sitting on one of the many old burial mounds. What their history, I do not know; but the vagueness has a certain charm about it. There is not a living being in sight, nor a sound—if I listen very attentively, I fancy I can just catch the faint echo of the sheep-bells of some flock in the far distance. The flowers are all beautiful in their freshness, it is useless gathering them—they so soon wither. What a blessing that the memory of them will last !

" I broke off in my letter this morning at Broadlands, I was going to tell you of the gracious reception given to the many excursionists. Lord and Lady Mount Temple themselves led the groups, amounting to a crowd, through their beautiful rooms and then into the garden and into the orangery, where refreshments were served with most generous ordering of things. Such gracious kindness to strangers I never saw shown, both in word and deed. I was asked to take part in thanking Lord and Lady Mount Temple, in the name of the rest, but I declined taking so prominent a position, for the reason that I felt quite sure there were there others who could and who would do it better than I, and I was most anxious that it should be well done. I was not there even to hear the vote of thanks, but was away taking a walk by the riverside and among the trees, and so I missed this part of the proceedings, but I heard Lord Mount Temple acknowledge their spoken thanks in a beautiful little speech. He said he greatly delighted in the charm of the place and that he felt that Providence had been very bountiful to him in placing him in a position to enjoy it so continually—and that, mixed with his pleasure, came the fear that he might be too selfish in his enjoyment of it, and out of that the desire grew that others should share it with him—and hence he was always glad to see visitors and excursionists from the neighbourhood, and he even thanked them for coming, for *their* pleasure in what was so beautiful to him made *his* enjoyment and pleasure in it all the greater."

SWAN UNITED ELECTRIC LIGHTING CO.,
August 29*th,* 1882.

To H. S.

" I have just arrived from Southampton. I have not enjoyed the B.A. meetings. I seemed to have no work to do, and that is unsatisfactory. As to pleasure, you know that, English-like, I take my pleasures sadly. I am not good at pleasure, at least not at the pleasure of mixing with a crowd. I went as a duty and chiefly to see Sir Wm. Thomson and, as you know, I saw him. I must say in qualification of what I have been saying, in a half grumbling tone, that I met with great kindness from everybody I came in contact with."

In consequence of the formation of the Edison & Swan Company, with its headquarters and its principal works in London,[1] the chief sphere of Swan's activities was now shifted from the north to the south. London required more of his time ; and it became clear that in order to keep closely in touch with the important developments in electric lighting which were then in progress, he must leave the Tyne and find a house in the south within easy reach of London. His search took him first to the neighbourhood of Hampton Court and Richmond, but finding nothing to his liking there beyond the historic associations of the place, he went farther afield. At Epsom he visited a house whose history connected it with the Prince Regent; " but," he writes, " I don't like the George IV. associations. I am a baby in such fancies. I heard a great deal about the house ; among other things, that it is ' haunted.'

[1] The main lamp factory was at this time set up at Ponders End.

How do you like that ?   Would you find it pleasant to have ' your own name in corners cried, when the shiver of dancing leaves is thrown about its echoing chambers wide ? '   The little town seems clean and pleasant, if a trifle ' horsey '."

Finally his search took him to Kent and to Bromley.

GREAT NORTHERN HOTEL,
September 10*th*, 1882.

To H. S.

" I must say I think the Bromley neighbourhood most delightful, and I had a good view of it for I took a carriage and postboy and drove from Bromley to Eltham, nine miles through the most delightful country ;

> ' Thro' the green lanes of Kent,
>   Green sunny lanes
>   Where groups of children laugh
>   And gather daisies.'

It was a lovely drive !   I wish you had been with me."

And so Bromley was chosen for the future home.

CHAPTER VII

A HOME IN THE SOUTH: FURTHER INVENTIONS: THE
MINERS' LAMP: ARTIFICIAL SILK: COPPER DEPOSITION

EARLY in 1883 the Swan family moved south to take possession of their new home, " Lauriston," at Bromley, a little Kentish town which at that time still kept its rural character and open surroundings, as the large estates in the neighbourhood were only beginning to be broken up. " Lauriston " stood on the extreme north-west fringe of the town, its gates opening upon the old coach road which ran through Lewisham to London. It was a newly built, good-sized house with some three acres of ground in which grew many old trees. The garden was re-planned by John Hancock in a simple and natural way, and became a place of many pleasures at all seasons of the year, from the earliest spring flowers till on the long south wall peaches and plums hung warm and ripe behind a fore-ground of autumn flowers. In hard winters the tennis lawn was turned into a skating-rink, the sheet of ice being gradually formed and thickened by repeated sprink-lings, as ice-rinks are formed in Switzerland. By these means an excellent surface was obtained, and much enjoyed by the Swan children and their friends for skating at night. An arc lamp was rigged up to light the scene, and Swan (no skater himself), looking like a big Father Christmas with flowing white beard and a great fur coat, dispensed hot coffee and soup to the skaters from an improvised buffet.

Across the London Road, nearly opposite to "Lauriston," stands the fine old college built by a Bishop of Rochester in Charles II.'s reign—a haven of rest for the widows and daughters of poor clergymen. The rich mellow colouring of the brick and stone work in its setting of lawns and ancient trees, seen through the wrought iron gates (their stone pillars crowned with Bishop's mitres), makes a picture that would have delighted the heart of Frederick

Walker.   Outside its walls was the ample glebe, since sold to augment the college funds, and now covered with rows of houses.

The narrow streets of the little town belong to the age of the coach and the post-chaise.   There were two fine old inns, one of which, "The Bell," has the distinction of having been recommended by Lady Catharine de Burgh to Elizabeth Bennett when she drove from Westerham to London.   The Bishops of Rochester had their palace in Bromley, a stately house, approached by a long avenue of elms, and standing in a fair demesne, now, alas, clipped for building.

To the newcomers from the grey, striving north there was a great charm in this picturesque little town.   In the kindlier climate of the south all growing things, both children and plants, seemed to thrive with less of an effort than at Low Fell, where the smoke of chemical works and pits and the blight of the bleak north-easter make the struggle for life more stern and the conditions of living more rigorous.

The country round about Bromley was picturesque and interesting, and Swan liked nothing better than a holiday drive, with a carriage full of children, over the neighbouring commons of Hayes, Keston, Chislehurst, and the Crays. A letter written to his daughter, then in Capri, gives a characteristic description of his enjoyment of these drives:

"I suppose it is pretty hot in Capri by this time, because here, in cold misty England even, it is not merely warm, but hot!   And the gardens and the orchards! You should see them to know what they look like, for they are beyond description.   We have been a long drive this afternoon, by St Paul's Cray, Lock's Bottom, and round by Hayes, and home by Pickhurst Mead.   To use the invariable descriptive phrase of Osborne,[1] 'the trees is littally smoffered with bloom,' and so they are.   The white and red of the apple and pear trees is the only colour to be seen.   It is a wonderful season, I never

---

[1] The gardener.

remember one so hot at this season, nor so beautiful in every way. The cuckoo is here, and the nightingale. It is full summer in fact, so far as the temperature goes; and delicious late spring so far as the trees are suggestive of the season. ' The brushwood sheaf round the elm tree's bole is in tiny leaf,' and has been for a fortnight. As we drove across the commons covered with gorse in flower, the ground dry and the air warm, it seemed it would be the very ideal of physical enjoyment to lie down on the dry grass among the gorse and contemplate ' the blue liberality of heaven,' or fall asleep there."

The song of the nightingale had for him a special attraction, partly perhaps owing to its rarity and unfamiliarity to one born and bred in the north country. A favourite springtime quest was to seek out the haunts of the nightingale and then, in charmed silence, to listen for those sudden thrilling bursts of rhapsody, and the distant note of the answering song.

"Lauriston," though a roomy enough house for ordinary purposes, had no accommodation for laboratory or experimental work. Accordingly a small adjacent house called " Sunnyside," whose garden communicated with " Lauriston," was acquired, and a chemical laboratory was fitted up in the lower part, the rest of the house being used as a kindergarten where the younger members of the Swan family, together with the children of a few neighbours, received elementary schooling. Between " Lauriston " and " Sunnyside " an additional building was erected for such experimental work as required more space than "Sunnyside" afforded. There was also another building put up to serve in part as a workshop, where one or two mechanics were employed, and in part as an engine-house; for " Lauriston " was, of course, lighted with the incandescent electric light, and the electricity had to be generated on the spot. This was done by means of a gas-engine and dynamo. The latter, a machine of Swan's own design and (except for the castings) entirely constructed in his workshop on the premises, was used

G

to charge a large battery of secondary cells, from which the current for lighting was drawn.

One of the first pieces of experimental work to which Swan devoted himself after his removal to Bromley was the improvement of the carbon filament for the lamp. Up to the end of 1883 the method of making the carbon filament which held the field was that which he had devised in 1880, namely, the carbonization of parchmentized cotton thread. But he was not satisfied with this method. He saw the possibility of getting a filament of greater uniformity and efficiency by making a non-fibrous thread expressly for this purpose. This led him, towards the end of 1883, to devise a new principle and method of filament manufacture, which very soon superseded the parchmentized thread process.

According to the new method, which he patented,[1] nitro-cellulose dissolved in acetic acid was squirted, or discharged under slight pressure, through a die or small orifice into a coagulating fluid, e.g., methylated spirit, so as to form a continuous homogeneous thread of indefinite length. This coagulated thread, after being washed and denitrated with ammonium sulphide, was then cut and shaped to the desired length and form, and carbonized in the usual manner.

As the result of the introduction of the squirting process, filaments could be made of far greater uniformity and fineness than formerly, and consequently it became possible to produce lamps of comparatively low candle-power for higher voltages. The advantage and economy thus gained greatly extended the use of incandescent electric lighting, and this principle of filament manufacture soon became universal, and has ever since continued to be the standard method of carbon filament manufacture.

Shortly after Swan had devised his squirting process, Mr. Legh S. Powell independently devised an alternative process in which cellulose dissolved in chloride of zinc was similarly squirted and carbonized. In 1888 Mr.

[1] Patent No. 5978 of 1883.

Powell demonstrated his process to Swan, who thereupon invited him to pursue some further researches in his laboratory at " Sunnyside," and collaborate with him in further improvement of the squirting process of filament manufacture. Mr. Powell accepted the invitation, and continued for some months working on this and other experimental ideas which were also at that time engrossing Swan's attention, relating more particularly to the rapid electrolytic deposition of copper.

It was during his early experimentation with the squirting process that Swan conceived the idea that the thread-like material, designed for filaments, was also capable of being used in a textile way for the manufacture of a fabric. With this object in view he produced threads of special fineness, not comparable, of course, to the fineness of the natural silk from the cocoon, or of the artificial silk of to-day, but as fine as could be obtained with the means he had then available.

Some of the finer cellulose threads produced in this way were crocheted by his wife into lace and used to make the border of small mats and doyleys. A few of these articles were exhibited at the Inventions Exhibition of 1885, under the description " artificial silk."

In this application of the squirted cellulose thread lay the germ of one of the most important inventions of modern times, the artificial silk manufacture. Swan did not, however, pursue the idea beyond the elementary stage. The task of developing it was left for others, and it is interesting to record that amongst the principal pioneers who succeeded in working out a practical process of making artificial silk from squirted cellulose was Charles Stearn, Swan's ingenious collaborator in the genesis of the incandescent electric lamp.

The cellulose, however, with which Stearn made his artificial silk was not the nitro-cellulose which Swan had used for his artificial silk, but " viscose," another form of cellulose, chemically known as cellulose xanthate.[1]

[1] The invention of Cross, Bevan, and Beadle; Patent No. 8700 of 1892.

And thereby hangs a tale which shows how intimately associated with the genesis and development of the artificial silk industry have been the inventor of the incandescent carbon filament lamp and his assistants.

Mr. Swinburne[1] has supplied the following interesting piece of history with reference to the " viscose " basis of artificial silk manufacture. About 1899, shortly after Stearn had commenced the manufacture of carbon filament lamps at Kew, Swinburne met him and asked him how he made his filaments. Stearn told him, " from chloride of zinc solution of cellulose." " Why don't you try viscose ? " suggested Swinburne, " it is much less tricky to work." After a few months Stearn came back with a reel of filament made from viscose. Swinburne had seen in the Inventions Exhibition of 1885 Swan's exhibit of artificial silk made from carbon filament material, and possibly some recollection of it passed through his mind and prompted the further suggestion, " Why don't you make *artificial silk* of viscose ? " Stearn did not know anything about artificial silk manufacture ; so the Chardonnet[2] process was explained to him. In a month or two he came back to show Swinburne a beautiful sample of viscose artificial silk, and offered Swinburne a share in the syndicate he was starting to work the process. After carrying on the manufacture for a short time, the syndicate was taken over by Messrs. Courtaulds, and this was the beginning of the enormous industry which that enterprising firm has so successfully developed.

A material contribution to the success of Stearn's manufacture of artificial silk from viscose was the inven-

---

[1] See page 82.

[2] Count Hilaire de Chardonnet, the inventor and pioneer of artificial silk manufacture in France. His process, patented in 1884 (a year after Swan's patent for squirting nitro-cellulose), consisted in extruding, under pressure, a solution of nitro-cellulose through capillary orifices, and subsequent treatment of the filament to render it suitable for textile use. Specimens of artificial silk fabric made by Chardonnet's process were shown at the Paris Exhibition of 1889.

tion of the " spinning box " by Fred Topham, who, as a young glass-blower employed by Stearn in Birkenhead, had made the bulbs for the first Swan lamps, and had remained with Stearn to assist him in the manufacture of lamps and, ultimately, of artificial silk.

Before leaving the subject of the carbon filament to speak of Swan's other experimental work, it will be convenient to refer at this point to the important litigation upon which the Edison & Swan Company embarked in 1885, in order to restrain infringement and maintain their patent monopoly in the manufacture of the carbon filament lamp. It was in the course of this litigation that the position of Swan and Edison in regard to priority of invention came under judicial consideration.

Mention has already been made of the fact that Swan had publicly exhibited his lamp in December 1878 and on several occasions in 1879 before the date of Edison's British patent of November 1879. This patent had, in consequence of the amalgamation, become the property of the Edison & Swan Company and, on account of its exceedingly broad and fundamental claims, gave the company, if the patent could be sustained, a very valuable monopoly. Infringers, or would-be infringers, however, were not slow to perceive that these prior public demonstrations by Swan might be used as a means of invalidating Edison's patent, on the ground of what in legal phrase is known as a " prior user." The company was consequently placed in a somewhat awkward predicament. So far as the invention and development of a practical form of incandescent lamp in this country and the actual processes necessary for its successful manufacture were concerned, they owed practically everything to Swan and practically nothing to Edison ; but so far as the maintenance of their patent monopoly was concerned, Edison's patent was of the utmost value to them. To retain this patent and preserve the monopoly it assured was a matter of paramount importance to them. In order to achieve this, it became necessary for the company to satisfy the Court either that the lamps shown by Swan in 1878 and 1879 were unsuccessful experiments, or that they were not incandescent lamps containing a *carbon filament*, for Edison's claims mentioned a carbon filament as an essential feature.

Both these lines of argument were urged with all the adroitness, persuasiveness and ingenuity that the eminent patent counsel retained for the company could employ. The latter argument, however, proved the more effectual, and the crucial question arose : Was the carbon conductor in the Swan lamp of 1879 a filament, or was it not ? If it *was* a filament, then Edison's patent was bad, by reason of Swan's prior user. If it was not a filament, then the situation was saved. After listening to evidence and argument which lasted many days, the Court of Appeal arrived at the conclusion that the carbon conductor in the Swan lamp was *not* a filament. So the company succeeded in saving the patent and securing the maintenance of its monopoly. But this triumph was not achieved without some incidental diminution of the credit justly due to the inventor on whose original work their successful manufacture of the incandescent electric lamp was in the main actually founded.

Swan was uniformly happy in the choice of assistants for his laboratory work. Mr. Legh S. Powell, to whom allusion has been made in connection with the development of the squirting process, was succeeded in 1892 by John Rhodin, a clever young Swedish chemist, fresh from the University of Upsala. Swan had already for some months past been engaged in researches relating to the electrolytic deposition of copper, and into the continuation of these researches Rhodin entered with enthusiasm, and proved himself a most skilful and helpful assistant.

Swan had the gift of arousing the enthusiasm of his assistants. He was always ready to listen to their ideas as well as to advance his own. He took them completely into his confidence. They were welcome at any time of day or night to come and discuss with him the progress of experiments, and the drawing-room was almost as commonly the scene of these discussions as the laboratory. In the researches in which Rhodin now joined him Swan had several objects in view.

One was to discover the precise conditions which controlled the speed and character of the electrolytic deposition of copper, with a view to obtaining a more rapid and regular deposit than was commonly obtainable at that date.

Another object was to obtain a copper deposit having the elastic and tough quality of wrought copper—in other words, to suppress the tendency of the electrolytic deposit to assume a crystalline structure resembling cast rather than wrought metal. A further object was to devise a more efficient and economical method than that in common use for producing copper wire of the high degree of purity and conductivity requisite for electrical work. The usual procedure at that time was to deposit copper electrolytically upon the cathode, and then melt up the copper so deposited in order to put it in a form convenient for the market and for rolling and drawing. This additional operation adds to the cost, and somewhat diminishes the purity of the copper.

This is not the place to recall in detail the course of the experiments bearing on these problems. Those who desire a more technically complete and precise account of this interesting series of researches, will find it in the joint communication by Swan and Rhodin to the Royal Society.[1]

Suffice it here to say that many of the observations made and conclusions arrived at in the course of these experiments have proved of permanent practical value in the industry concerned with the electrolytic deposition of metals. A few of these novel observations may be summarized.

Swan found that under proper conditions it was pos-

[1] *Transactions*, Royal Society, 1894.

sible to obtain tough copper with a current density ranging from 1 ampère to 1000 ampères per square foot of cathode surface. The conditions necessary to obtain the desired result were : (*a*) the adaptation of the strength of the solution to the strength of the current, using the strongest solution with the largest current ; and (*b*) rapid circulation of the electrolyte when the current density was high.

He found that regularity and smoothness of deposit were almost entirely dependent on the absence of solid particles held in suspension in the electrolyte, and that excrescences could be entirely avoided by taking care that the electrolyte was free from solid floating particles.

He found, also, that an exceedingly rapid flow of the electrolyte over the cathode surface tended to suppress the crystalline condition of the deposit.

He found that, by modifying the bath and by actively stirring it during deposition, good copper could be deposited fifty times faster than the common rate.

Applying the knowledge thus acquired to the continuous production of copper wire, he worked out a process in which a copper wire stretched in an electrolytic bath was, whilst receiving a deposit of copper, continually subjected to the action of wire draw-plates. This resulted in the unlimited extension of the wire without increase of its thickness, all the deposit going to increase the length. Thus the original wire formed a core which, as the process proceeded, dwindled towards nothing.

The process was worked successfully on a large experimental scale. But the output of wire was small relatively to the size of the apparatus, and he was forced to the conclusion that the gain of 1 per cent. or 2 per cent. in the conductivity of the wire would be outweighed by the disproportionately high cost of the plant required. The method was practicable but uncommercial.

An instance of an observation of considerable practical utility arising from these investigations may be mentioned, as it affords an illustration of that type of discovery which springs from some unforeseen and purely fortuitous occurrence in the course of experimentation.

Swan was working with a hot solution of nickel, and up to a certain point the deposit had the usual dead grey appearance. Suddenly, and without doing anything more than putting in a new cathode, he found that the character of the deposit had completely changed. Instead of the grey, tough, adherent deposit, there was produced a brittle, specular deposit, which scaled off in brilliantly shining flakes of metal. It was some time before the cause of this extraordinary change could be discovered. It was eventually traced to the accidental introduction into the solution of a minute quantity of glue, dissolved from the bristles of one of the burnishing brushes.

Consequent upon this discovery, he found that by adding a small amount of gelatine or similar organic material to a nickel or copper solution he could obtain the peculiar bright and brittle deposit that had resulted from this accident.

This means of modifying the character of the deposited metal has since become everyday practice in electro-metallurgical operations where a deposit of this character is desired.

Such, in outline, was the more important experimental work with which Swan was occupied during his residence at Bromley. As for his other activities, his goings and comings, and the various interests and incidents of this period of his life, one cannot do better than give some account of them in the characteristic language of his own letters.

CHAPTER VIII

LETTERS

In the spring of 1885 some business concerning patents took Swan to Germany. After visiting a lamp factory that had been recently started at Kalk, two miles from Cologne, under the management of Charles Stearn, he proceeded with Stearn to Berlin. They found the city *en fête* for the Emperor's birthday.

He writes from the Hotel de Rome, March 22nd, 1885, to his wife, whom with two of the children he had escorted as far as Paris on her way to Arcachon.

" It is an unfortunate day for the crowds that throng the streets. A heavy shower of snow and hail is now falling, and similar showers, chiefly hail, have fallen during the whole day at short intervals, in some of which the sunshine broke through the clouds and shone with a fitful but welcome glare for a few minutes. We meant to have gone to the cathedral where the Emperor and all the Court went in state, but we were too late to get any place worth keeping, and so we formed undistinguished items in the throng which lined the streets and waited with more or less patience to catch a glimpse of the occupants of the gay carriages as they passed. I did not see the Emperor in a way to recognize him—but I saw the Crown Prince, the Prince of Wales, and some of the other princes. I also saw Count von Moltke. The service was over before 12, and on the return journey there was again a chance of seeing the great people. I am afraid we did not make as much of our opportunity as we might. It is a tedious business waiting to see a carriage pass, and not satisfying in the end. We went to see the Museum of Sculpture and Painting. I was much interested in the pictures—renewing my slight acquaintance with the Old Masters. Murillo, Rembrandt, Rubens, Vandyk, Velasquez, Titian are all well represented. There are some very fine portraits by Franz Hals, and I think

the most charming Greuze I ever saw is here. But I
could not stay long enough to enjoy them thoroughly.
It is the worst of flying visits to galleries, you cannot
examine the pictures critically as they deserve to be
examined. On the whole, I was surprised to find so
excellent a collection. The Museum building is a very
fine one, both as regards the front elevation and the
interior arrangements."

During this visit to Germany he records with appreciation two family parties at which he was present, especially one—a birthday party at the house of his old friend,
Herr Schmidt of Barmen—where he much enjoyed the
cordiality and jollity of the family life. " The simple
unaffected friendliness of the members of the family to
each other was something that we only see, or used to see,
in old village life in England. The laughing and chatter
were almost deafening, and full of good nature."

The tedium of the homeward journey was relieved by
Adam Bede. He writes from Cologne on March 29th,
1885. " I am going to send you the second volume of
Adam Bede. The detail of the pictures so charms in the
first volume that the interest in the drama is scarcely
greater than the interest you feel in these details—Mrs.
Poyser's wonderfully pithy sayings and the lovely picture
of Dinah. But in the second volume the tragedy is so
absorbing in its grim progress that you cannot bestow
the same attention on the detail of it. The truth of
the story is absolute, it is nature itself! A miracle of a
woman, George Eliot!"

He returned via Brussels, much admiring the " pretty
clean little city," and recalling that it was the city in
which Charlotte Brontë was at school, and in which some
of the scenes of *Villette* and *The Professor* were laid.

After a hurried visit to the north to attend to his
various business interests there, he betook himself to
Paris again, at the time of Victor Hugo's national funeral.
He writes from there on May 1st, 1885 :

" You see I have discovered the store of paper you

provided me with, and now you are to have the use of
the discovery.

"Beaufils came at nine this morning, and I went with
him to try and see the plate-coating, but the labour was
lost. No factories nor even the theatres are open in Paris
to-day. Paris is in its deepest mourning, which perhaps is
not saying much that conveys an idea of mourning at all;
for if it be true that the English take their pleasure sadly,
it seems to me, judging by the spectacle to-day, that it
may with equal truth be said that the French take their
mourning gaily. The funeral procession itself was a
Lord Mayor's Show with a dash of crêpe in it, not that
crêpe covered everything. There was plenty of gay colour
in the dresses of the soldiery, of which there was a strong
force, and in the flags and even in the gigantic wreaths
of flowers ; the prevailing colour of these floral circles,
some of which required four men to carry them, was
yellow. Then there was the booming of the cannon and
the blare of trumpets, and mingled with these and over-
powering the last at a little distance, the voice of the
crowd—truly 'the masses'—the millions of men and
women who gazed and chattered and laughed with an
abandon truly French. I was not very near to the line
of the procession, and what I have said of the crowd, near
where I was, may not be true of the crowd immediately
bordering on the line of the procession. I was content
to sit and stand by turns in my carriage, and look on from
a respectful distance—the distance in fact of the next
bridge to that over which the procession passed. The
procession consisted of various corporations or their
representatives : the Governmental, the Municipal,
the Military, the National, the Literary, etc., etc. ; and
interspersed among these various groups were triumphal
cars laden with flowers and flower wreaths, and crowned
with flag trophies. I did not wait to see the very end,
but after the plain hearse which bore the pauper's coffin
containing the body of the hero had passed, I got out of
the throng as soon as possible, for I had during the time

of waiting given a seat in the carriage to an old work-man who fainted in the crowd, or rather on the outer skirt of the crowd close beside me. I noticed him just before he sank down helpless; I felt sure he was ill. After he was lifted into my carriage and arranged in a comfort-able position, with his shirt-neck loosened (he had on a clean but much worn shirt and terribly patched but clean and not ragged clothes), a woman in the crowd brought out of her pocket a phial of sulphuric ether, and somebody else (I think a surgeon) a nob of sugar, and with these helps to the efforts of nature at a very low ebb he came to consciousness.

"He was so dazed and exhausted that I felt it would never do to leave him to get home on his legs, so I asked him where he lived, with a view to take him home in the carriage. He fumbled feebly in his pocket, and brought out an apology for a pocket-book in the form of several folds, one over the other in regular order, of brown paper, and inside these a few leaves of ruled writing paper, and on one of these his address neatly written and in full. It was a long way off—at Menilmontant on the remotest outskirt of Paris, but I wanted to see him safe home, and to see also what kind of home he had, so as soon as the crowd was so far satisfied with what one, I heard speak of it, called 'une belle démonstration' to somewhat clear a way, I went with my still silent and drooping charge toward Menilmontant. On the way we called at a restaurant and gave him some lemonade with a little brandy in it. It revived him very little, and as we went along I felt a strong and stronger conviction that food was the kind of stimulant he required. He was a nice-looking old man. Seventy-two he said he was, with an expression not unlike that of the old woman in Herkomer's picture of *Patience* in one of the magazines—the mouth somewhat fallen in for want of teeth. He looked as most of the poor, hardworking people do—older than his years. His hands showed all the signs of hard labour, but they were clean—one of the thumbs, I noticed, had been crushed. After a drive of almost an hour, and passing through some of the poorest streets of Paris, we reached the old man's home. The old wife came out to meet him and gently stroked his back as she guided him into their room, with two or three sympathizing neighbour wives about her—so far—but they did not go in. I went in—the old woman asked me to go in—and when the old man was seated in his chair, the tears came into his eyes as he thanked me. I was pleased to find evidences of cleanliness and comfort so far as the furnishing of the room went. There was a nice-looking bed and chairs and tables—all very simple, such as one sees in the English farm cottage. I found on inquiry that the old man was out of work. His only child, a daughter (with three children), could not help him much. An only son had been killed in the Prussian War. So I had not been far wrong in my forecast of the position. I gave the old woman—she was seventy-five—5 francs to buy some food with, and said good-bye. How strange it is to meet with people in that way just once and never to meet them again! I then went to see the pleasure-grounds of Chaumont, not far off, and which I had too imperfectly seen on my last visit. I wanted to see if the poor people and their children went there and used them as their own, and I was glad to see so many of the real working class were there with their wives and children, withdrawn for a few hours from the living tomb of a city and in contact with and drinking in the very breath of nature, surrounded by lovely trees and grass and flowers, with the sound of rippling water in their ears instead of the noise of the streets, and above, the blue height of heaven, as it is here in all its excellence. Then I descended physically from the heights of this delightful place (truly 'the desert made to blossom as the rose'), and mentally from my reflections on it, to the lower level of the boulevards and the commonplace of eating and drinking, dismissing a very typical shiny white-hatted Parisian *cocher* with 5 hours' pay before going into the restaurant of the Hotel du Nord. Thereafter I hired another carriage and drove to the Bois du Boulogne, passing the Arc du Triomphe on the way and having a good look at the funeral trappings which were still undisturbed, except by the wind. I found them very tawdry—well enough conceived but very badly executed. The great raised coffer which contained the coffin was well proportioned to the Arch, but the detail quite in the style of Birmingham at its worst. You will doubtless see it in the *Graphic* next week, and there it will not look ill, as I noticed it did not in reality, when you only saw it from a distance. I think it was a very good idea to use the Arch for this purpose, and it evidently pleased the Parisians completely. I heard a gentleman say that he had never enjoyed a funeral so much in his life, and I am certain he said what thousands have felt. Then I went to the Garden of Acclimatization and found it rather dreary, and I was glad to leave it and come to my hotel, where I found dinner waiting. After that too lengthy meal I came here to write this, which has long since exceeded all reasonable length, and now I must not and will not tax your patience, great as I know it to be, any more, but say as they say in Paris, Adieu ! ' "

In 1885–6 much of his time was taken up in demonstrating and making trials of his miner's electric lamp. One of his journeys to the north for this purpose is recorded in a letter from Mrs. Mawson's house, " Ashfield," dated December 13th, 1885 :

" We have just finished our late breakfast with its pleasant accompaniment of genial talk flowing almost uninterruptedly from the head of the table—talk of business—talk of politics—talk of public persons—talk of friends—talk of family affairs. Beginning not early and protracting the dual process of feeding body and mind at the same time, it is no wonder that we find the morning pretty well advanced before the meal is over. It is just over and it is just eleven, and my first duty, and

at the same time, pleasure, is to tell you of my welfare
and to acknowledge your letter. As I told you in the
few lines I wrote from Mosley Street the reading of my
paper [1] was well received. Numerous questions were
asked afterwards, and these I answered as well as I could,
and I think sufficiently well. The President, Mr.
Daglish, is anxious to have a lamp or two to try as
soon as possible. Prof. Connett, head of the College of
Physical Science here, is lecturing to pitmen at Cram-
lington (a pit village) to-morrow, and will take one of the
lamps to show the miners. Almost more interest was
manifested in the primary battery [2] than in the secondary
battery. When I get back, I must push on with my
experiments to simplify and lighten the battery. I
think two cells will do quite well and that six instead
of nine lbs. will be the weight one may reasonably
expect to come to. I must also try my hand to find a
good and simple indicator of fire-damp to attach to
the lamp. That would—if it can be done—make the
lamp perfect, if one may take the general expression of
opinion at the meeting yesterday as authoritative on the
point."

After some months' further work a fire-damp indicator
had been added to the miner's lamp, and in a letter dated
August 31st, 1886, he describes a visit to the Orpeth
Busty pit near Birtley:

" It was a most interesting excursion. There were four
in our party ; each had an electric lamp ; there were
two Marsaut lamps carried as well for comparison, and
very greatly the electric lamps beat them. We went to
three of the places where coal was being hewn and very
much astonished the hewers by the brilliance of our light.
It was ' like sunshine,' ' as leet as at bank,' ' By gosh !
noo, ef au hed a leet like that, au *wad* screen the coal ! '

---

[1] On the miner's lamp.

[2] A neatly designed voltaic cell, capable of generating sufficient current
to light a small lamp and so be of service on occasions when, through
accident or otherwise, no facilities existed for charging a secondary battery.

We failed to get any indication of ' gas,' the ventilation was so good; although we could hear and see the gas oozing out of the coal. I was down about two hours—over half a mile from the shaft, which is 700 feet deep. It was very hot, but otherwise not nearly so uncomfortable as in other pits where I have been."

Swan lost no opportunity of calling public attention to the greater degree of safety to be got by the use of electric light in coal mining. Hearing that Thomas Burt was calling the attention of Parliament to the " unsafety of the Davy lamp," he persuaded him to come to " Lauriston " to see this new safety lamp.

Early in 1886 he lectured on his miner's lamp in Glasgow and had the pleasure of discussing its latest features with Sir Wm. Thomson, and in August of that year he took the same subject for an address at the British Association Meeting in Birmingham. There he records his spending a pleasant day with " that dear old man " James Nasmyth, and his first meeting with Dr. Gore, an eminent physicist and electrician.

September 5th, 1886.

" I spent most part of yesterday in company with Dr. Gore—a very clever and very peculiar man who leads a very solitary life, pursuing physical studies of an original kind with great, I may say, *immense* industry and no less skill. We went together to the Hampstead Colliery and down that very deep pit—it is 2000 ft. deep—and about a mile into the workings. There was a pretty large party, among whom was Jesse Collings, M.P., and one or two others whom I knew. Richard Chamberlain, the brother of Joseph, was the guide of the party. I had my lamp with me. There is no gas in the mine, and consequently large open lights can be used in it; and yesterday there was no lack of light, for candles and lamps were stuck about everywhere. I was much interested in seeing the difference between the working here and in the north

H

country pits. Here the seam is 24 ft. thick! and this allows a totally different method of 'getting' the coal, by first excavating at the bottom of the seam and then working upwards to the top of it. The process consists in cutting in the coal-roof deep trenches or upward-tending well-holes close together, so that they form a trench by their side-junction with each other. The lines of trenches are shaped so as to encircle a space of roof and in effect insulate it. The insulated portion (often of great size—perhaps 6 ft. thick by 12 ft. square), thus deprived of support from the sides of the cutting, then simply falls down by its own weight in a great mass. I saw a fall produced, and the mass of coal detached from the roof was near 100 tons. In this case, to ensure the fall taking place while we were there, a couple of bore-holes were blasted. These made the not 'too solid earth' reverberate and tremble. I am glad you were not there, and hear only a *description* of it instead of *it*."

Swan had always a thirst for new knowledge, and accordingly welcomed and enjoyed the opportunities which these gatherings gave him for meeting his many scientific friends and discussing with them his own and their special problems ; by turns gleaning useful information and imparting it. But for the social functions, the receptions and conversaziones that accompanied these scientific meetings, he had little relish. He found them tiring and tedious. Though an interesting talker on subjects that interested him, he was no conversationalist. He preferred a quiet uninterrupted talk with a friend or two rather than the somewhat desultory and dilettante conversation of the soirée. With his wife beside him— and she accompanied him whenever possible on these occasions—these functions were less irksome, for he enjoyed her evident enjoyment of them. But without her sociable and stimulating company he found them, as a rule, uncongenial.

He writes :

" With a distracting buzz of talk going on about me, I make the attempt to tell you where I am and what I have been doing—as to what I am going to do, I will be reserved, for you know how dearly I love to retain my liberty of action, even to the last minute.

" The heading of my letter speaks for itself, as to the first point. As to the second, I occupied my time yesterday in getting my lamp cells put right and I am glad to say I succeeded. I got them charged at the Bingley Hall exhibition, and at the conversazione held there last night, which I attended, I saw they were all right, and I was able to show the lamps to a good many people during the evening. It was a very grand affair given by the Mayor and Corporation. During the evening I met a number of old friends and a number of new ones. The place was very gay and crowded ; but I was preoccupied with my lamps and, what is more than that, I had not you with me, and for these two reasons, and chiefly the last, I found the music and the light and the sound of many voices not exhilarating, but rather something like a dream panorama in which scenic effects were being unfolded before me, and I saw them as in a dream."

No quotation from his letters would be adequate which failed to convey an impression of the great comfort and assistance which his wife's companionship was to him both in his work and his recreation. Unfortunately, during this period, ill-health necessitated her being a good deal abroad at various health-resorts on the Continent, and separation was, therefore, inevitable. In the winter of 1890 he writes to tell her how he has kept, in north-country fashion, the custom of " first-footing," to mark the entry of the New Year.

LAURISTON,
January 1st, 1890.

" The new date for the first time.   A very happy New
Year to you!   How greatly I shall miss you to-day I
cannot express but you can imagine, for I think it is the
first New Year's Day we have been apart since we were
married; and how many happy years does that not cover?
Thank God for His goodness to us! so far from our deserts.
I came in 'first foot' as usual.   I think nearly all the
household was awake.   Servants at 'Watch-Night Service.'   Mary and Hilda came down to greet me at the
incoming of the year, and we had tea and cake together.
I was not sleepy, and did not go to bed for an hour."

LAURISTON,
August 12th, 1891.

" It is 5 o'clock and I have just had a cup of tea, all
by myself.   I made it strong and sweet, to compensate
me, as far as compensation was within my power, for the
absence of loved companionship, and as I sat I read, oh,
so sadly! a biographical notice of Russell Lowell, published with his portrait in the *Pall Mall*.   He was a most
dear soul! and now I wish more than ever that I had
seen more of him.   I feel more and more the truth that
Tennyson utters when he says, ' There's something comes
to us in life, but more is taken quite away.'   The great
souls of the world seem to grow greater as they recede
from us, as the sun does at its setting.   Either I am out
of touch with the new men, or they are very inferior to
the old.   Who is there to replace Emerson, Longfellow,
and Lowell in America ?   Only Holmes, and he on the
edge of the all-embracing shadow—as is our own Tennyson.   It is a sad thing and I cannot help saying so, that
the passing of genius through life is so like the passing of
a shooting star through our atmosphere—coming out of
darkness, and quickly re-entering it again; and do what
we may, we cannot but repine at this hard law."

When at work in his laboratory, his letters to his wife kept her in close touch with the progress of his experiments.

Lauriston,
August 8th, 1891.

" I must write a line or two to tell you how dull the house looks without you or the children, and how I have been getting on with my wire operations.[1] The experience of yesterday was very similar to that of the day before. I had the apparatus going for about 3 hours, and then there was a breakdown of the sort that has often occurred before—a band broke, and the stoppage arising from this trifling accident put an end to continuance of the operation. It made a weak place in the wire that presently led to another breakdown of a less easily remediable kind, and so I had, after a very tiring day, to give up and rest ! I have done nothing at it to-day but plan how to avoid a recurrence of these failures, which are so annoying, because they are so nearly on the verge of complete success."

At this time Swan was interested in two engraving companies—the Meisenbach Co., of which he was a director, and the Swan Electric Engraving Co., which worked a photo-engraving process of his own invention under the direction of his eldest son. In connection with this work he made a journey to Germany and Austria, in order to confer with other experts in photogravure, with a view to effecting some improvement in the process.

Accompanied by his youngest son, he went first to Frankfort, where an electrical exhibition was being held. He writes from there on August 29th, 1891 : " The exhibition is an excellent one—more extensive and even more brilliant than that most delightful one that we enjoyed together ten years ago in Paris; and one experiences the same kind of elation that that created—the consequence,

[1] An experimental process, referred to on page 104, for the continuous drawing of copper wire.

I suppose, of the brilliant light and the crowd of objects of interest, and the crowd of eager examiners of them, and the music, and I may add also the dancing, for that also enters into the programme of the Frankfort Exhibition."

At the exhibition he met, among other scientific men, Dr. Hoeffner, the inventor of a copper-extracting process, Herr Schuckert of Nüremberg, and Dr. Müller, the designer of "that wonderful piece of electrical engineering—the transmission of 150 to 300 horse-power 108 miles by 3 small wires."

At Nüremberg they paid two visits to Schuckert's great works, "an immense place outside the town, where more dynamos are built than in any other place in Germany or in the world. The development of so new an industry as this in so short a time is wonderful, and we can, I fear, show nothing equal to it in England, the birthplace of the dynamo ; and that to me is a rather sad reflection."

In Vienna they visited the School of Photography and the Imperial Printing Offices, and he records that "at both places we have received most unbounded kindness and much information, some of which may prove useful."

From Prague he writes : "I felt myself free, after our business was finished, to spend the rest of the day in pleasure—and that I have been doing with as much diligence and labour as if it had been business. We had a carriage and a pair of horses all day, and drove to the different parts of the town to see the things most worthy to be seen, and we have had a very full day of it, finishing up with the Exhibition—for there is an Industrial Exhibition in Prague, and a very fine one too. We did not get there till 7 p.m. and then the chief attractions were the music and illuminated fountain, like that at South Kensington. There was a brilliant illumination by electric light—crowds of happy people, from old to very young, hundreds of school children among the rest, all enjoying —as southerners know best how—the gay sights and sounds and the delicious air, for after sunset the air became pleasantly cool after the scorching heat of the day—cool only by comparison with that.

"During the day, we have driven all over the city—been into two or three churches—among these, a Greek church and a Jews' synagogue, dating from the 8th or 9th century. We went through the Jews' quarter, a very interesting but a very dirty place that I was glad to escape from. One of the most interesting places we visited was the Vyshehrad, or Capitol of Prague. About it are grouped the Cathedral (in which the kings are crowned, and which is full of relics of old time), and the King's Palace or the Burg—into several of the rooms of which we were admitted. Some of these are magnificent, others both curious and magnificent; for instance, one immense room with a most intricate and beautiful roof—you may judge of its size when I tell you that tournaments used to be held in it. A very interesting room was a small council chamber in which the deliberations took place which produced the Thirty Years' War. It still contains the old furniture of that time, the tables and chairs being such as we see in very old paintings. The view of the city and river from the window at the end of this room is most beautiful. One's standpoint is a great height above the city, and its many towers and domes make a grand picture. Our guide told us that there were 105 towers in Prague, 60 churches and 8 bridges, and all these formed conspicuous objects in the view."

On the way home, after staying at Salzburg and Munich, they spent a day in Landsberg at Professor Herkomer's German home. "We had a long and interesting discussion (on etching principally) with the Professor. We watched him at work on a small plate which was to illustrate his new direct process at the lectures he is going to give at Oxford. A slight tracing had been previously made on the white etching ground, and he was making the complete drawing through this with the etching needle, while the model—a strong old Bavarian peasant—stood as firm as a rock. I went into the town of Landsberg with Siegfried,[1] and found it to be a very pretty old place—very stagnant and antiquated, but very picturesque. The river Lech—a rushing torrent to-day from recent rains—flows between Herkomer's house and the Mutterthurm and the town of Landsberg. The Mutterthurm is far more beautiful in reality than the photographs of it. The colour, principally depending on a very skilful use of coloured roof tiles, adds greatly to the effect.

In the autumn of 1891 Swan made another business visit to the north, and writes on October 15th :

" As you may imagine I have been living very fast since I came here ('Ashfield').[2] There was much to talk about, and we have been talking about it. Who do you think was our last visitor ? Why, William Stead, and didn't he talk and didn't we all talk, and often all together, a real ' clash,' chiefly about ghosts ! Stead is going to bring out a Christmas print on the subject, and wants 'matter.' "

In the early part of 1892 there is a series of letters written to his wife who was at Bordighera, while he was detained in England, chiefly occupied in reorganizing the dry-plate works at Low Fell with Mr. Stanley, an American expert in the manufacture of photographic plates, whose machines were being installed there.

On February 5th, 1892, he writes from Bromley before going north :

" I found your delightful note on my return from the Royal Institution lecture. I had time to go up into Professor Dewar's rooms and had the pleasure—the very great pleasure—of shaking hands with Tesla. He is a delightful fellow. We had a pleasant exchange of compliments. The lecture was like that of the previous evening, full of the most exciting and startling incidents. Everything is going on here as well as can be expected in your absence—indeed, things outward are unusually bright.

[1] Professor Hubert von Herkomer's son.

[2] "Ashfield" was the home of his eldest sister, Elizabeth Mawson, at Low Fell.

It is a glorious morning! but oh! the house is very quiet, and I am yet hardly accustomed to the reason of the general stillness. During breakfast I was expecting every moment the 'rest' would come down; but they never did, and so there was only 'we few, we . . . few' to eat it. The kitten is moping—I expect it misses you as everybody and everything in the house does."

February 7th, 1892.

" I am very glad to think of you as having achieved the long and arduous journey, and being now in, I trust, the full enjoyment of the fruits of it—warmth and sunshine. I went to the Royal Institution lecture yesterday afternoon, and was well repaid for the journey to town. I saw the great induction coil operated quite successfully, and a number of very beautiful experiments performed in the deftest manner by Dr Fleming, who acquitted himself as a lecturer with very great ability."

Shortly afterwards Swan himself delivered the Friday evening lecture at the Royal Institution, appropriately choosing as his topic "Electro-Metallurgy," a science which may be said to have been brought to birth within those very walls by Davy's historic demonstration of the electrolytic production of the alkali metals. In his lecture Swan reviewed the growth of the electro-metallurgical industry, and described and showed some of his own experiments, to which allusion has already been made, on the rapid deposition of copper.

This lecture was later repeated at Newcastle and at Birmingham.

CHAPTER IX

LIFE IN LONDON

IN 1894 Swan was elected a Fellow of the Royal Society, an honour which he prized above all others that his scientific work brought him. His election followed upon a communication to the Society recording the results of the elaborate research upon the electrolytic deposition of copper which he had carried out with the assistance of John Rhodin,[1] and to which allusion has already been made.

In the same year the family moved from Bromley to London, a change necessitated by increasingly numerous engagements in connection with learned societies and company business in which Swan found himself involved. Though the distance from London was but ten miles, the only available means of transit was the South Eastern and Chatham Railway, not famed in those days either for celerity or comfort ; and the constant travelling to and fro was found to be too fatiguing and wasteful of time.

Accordingly "Lauriston" was given up and 58, Holland Park was bought, a house large enough to accommodate the now almost grown-up family, and with spare rooms in the basement which could be fitted up as a chemical and physical laboratory and workshop.

During the years that followed the removal of the family to London Swan continued his experimental work ; but much of his time was absorbed in work of a public nature in connection with various scientific societies. He served on the Council of the Royal Society and was a visitor at the Royal Institution, and was also on the Board of the National Physical Laboratory. From 1898–9 he was President of the Institution of Electrical Engineers, and from 1900–1 President of the Society of Chemical Industry. In 1903 he was President of the Pharmaceutical Society, and in 1904 the Faraday Society chose him

---

[1] See page 103.

as their first President. He was Vice-President of the
Senate of University College, London, and was for many
years an active member of the council and committee of
management.

These offices were most congenial to him, bringing
him into contact with kindred spirits, with whom he
could work in full accord in the interests of scientific
progress and education. He had also at this time a good
deal of work to do as director of two public companies:
the Edison & Swan Electric Light Co., on whose
board he continued as long as his health permitted,
and the Notting Hill Electric Lighting Co., a recently
formed electricity supply company, of which two of his
scientific colleagues, Sir William Crookes and Col. R. E.
Crompton, were directors.

The board meetings of the latter company were sometimes held at the offices of his old friend, Sir Frederick
Bramwell, the consulting engineer and expert witness, in
whose company Swan always found that the tedium of
business was pleasantly relieved by "seeing his jovial
happy face and hearing his delicious voice."

The meetings of the Edison & Swan Co. lacked such
redeeming features, and Swan often found them exhausting and uncongenial, particularly when they involved, as
they sometimes did, a clash of opinion with men whose
commercial outlook underrated the urgent need, in a
business based on technical processes, for constant
research and experiment in order to keep abreast of or,
as Swan desired, a little in advance of the times. No
doubt there is justification for the diffident and cautious
attitude which some directors adopt towards the suggestions of an inventor on whose invention a manufacturing
business is based; for inventors are by no means always
sound guides on questions of manufacturing policy,
being, as a rule, too prone to make innovations that
disturb continuity and occasion expense out of proportion to the technical gain achieved. Swan, however,
had no such propensity; on the contrary he showed

great caution in introducing innovations. One of his younger colleagues[1] says, in commenting on this trait: "He acted rather on the principle underlying the French proverb ' le meilleur est l'ennemi du bon.' He refrained from suggesting small improvements which would disorder manufacture. He would say : 'That may not be perfect, but we know it works. Why make an alteration which, though it may be a little better, may introduce something that we do not foresee ? ' His policy always was to keep a manufacture going straight on without variation until he had evolved an improvement substantial enough to make it worth while to make a general change."

But Swan, although he was not hasty in pressing for the adoption of improvements, was constantly emphasizing the importance of a well-equipped experimental department as a necessary adjunct of the Edison & Swan Co.'s business. The important patents which had for so long secured this company a monopoly in the incandescent lamp manufacture had expired by 1897, and Swan saw clearly that it was only by most vigilant and industrious attention to the improvement of the lamp that the company could hold its own against the competition which threatened it. Much of the experimental work that he undertook in his private laboratory at Holland Park was devoted to this object; and to help the company still further he placed the services of his own laboratory assistant at their disposal to carry out researches at the works at Ponders End. His anxiety on this score is reflected in his letters. He writes on July 31st, 1898 :

"I am very much preoccupied with devices for the improvement of the electric lamp. For 18 years there has been no radical change in it, only such changes as arise from practice in manufacture. Now there are signs of radical and far-reaching change, and I am naturally anxious that these changes, if they do come,

[1] James Swinburne, F.R.S.

as I expect they will, may not find us unprepared for them, nor wholly unconnected with them. I am busy considering a patent specification."

Amongst the far-reaching changes alluded to in this letter was the substitution of a metallic filament for the carbon filament which until then had held the field. For some years past Swan had experimented intermittently with various refractory metals, tungsten amongst others, in the endeavour to obtain a more efficient filament. But in this endeavour he, together with the other English scientists at work on the same problem, was forestalled by German inventors. Baron Auer von Welsbach, the inventor of the gas mantle, was successful also in producing an incandescent electric lamp with a filament of the metal osmium. This was shortly afterwards followed by the tantalum filament lamp of Messrs. Siemens & Halske, and later by the sintered tungsten filament made by the Osram Company according to the invention of Just and Hanaman. The tungsten filament, greatly improved, and made now in the form of a ductile drawn wire, has gradually ousted the carbon filament, and is at present universally used wherever luminous efficiency is the primary consideration. The carbon filament lamp is, however, still manufactured, though only now for special purposes, as, for example, where heat rays as well as light rays are a desideratum.

There was also another business which claimed a share of Swan's attention, namely, the photo-engraving company in which his eldest son was engaged. This concern was started originally in 1885 as a partnership between Swan and Thomas Annan of Glasgow for the purpose of working the process of photogravure improved by Klic, and many fine works of art were produced at the firm's studio at Lambeth, under the supervision of J. Craig Annan and Donald Cameron-Swan, sons of the partners. In 1893, after the death of Thomas Annan and the withdrawal of his son to Glasgow, Donald was taken into partnership with his father, and the style of the firm was changed to " Swan Electric Engraving Company." The manufacture of " half tone " blocks was added to photogravure at the company's new premises in the Charing Cross Road, and eventually typographic printing from the " Swan-type " blocks was undertaken. A few years before his death Sir Joseph retired from an active share in the control of the business, but still continued to take a keen interest in the various processes operated at Charing Cross Road, contributing from time to time new ideas and suggestions for improved methods.

Swan's researches during this period were carried out with the assistance of A. C. Hyde, who had succeeded John Rhodin shortly before the departure from Bromley. Mr. Hyde, besides being an experienced and resourceful experimenter, had also himself an inventive turn of mind, and several inventions of practical value stand to his credit, notably the method of welding known as " Hyde Welding." This process takes advantage of the phenomenon (observed in the course of experiments conducted in Swan's laboratory) that hydrogen causes fused or semi-fused copper to spread over a metallic surface with a remarkable degree of mobility, so that if two surfaces of iron, for instance, are brought together with copper powder or shavings interposed, and then, in the presence of hydrogen, raised to the temperature at which copper normally begins to melt, the copper will run with extraordinary fluidity into all the interstices between the two opposed surfaces and at the same time slightly penetrate below the surface of the iron, thereby effecting a weld of a very complete and tenacious character.

The laboratory notebooks of these years reveal a great variety of experimental work undertaken mainly to solve some problem of immediate practical importance in connection with manufactures in which Swan was directly or indirectly interested, such as the improve-

Sɪʀ Joseph Wilson Swan, F.R.S., ɪɴ ʜɪs Laboratory ᴀᴛ Holland Park

ment of the incandescent lamp or the perfecting of those processes of photo-engraving which formed the basis of the business in which his eldest son was engaged. With no less keenness, however, did he initiate and carry through experiments to solve some difficulty or effect some improvement in processes in which he had no personal concern beyond the fact that friends or acquaintances had sought his advice and aroused his scientific interest.

There was also undertaken during this period an interesting series of experiments which have a considerable bearing on the construction of electrical transformers of the induction-coil type. The experiments were designed to elucidate various phenomena which Swan and his assistants had observed during their building of an exceptionally large induction coil. Whilst seeking for the best means of insulating the high tension portion of the coil, they noticed peculiar movements in the waxy materials used in the dielectric insulation, and it was with a view to ascertaining the exact nature of the electrical strains produced during the working of the coil in its dielectric parts that these researches were carried out.

In order to obtain a visual picture of the conditions which exist when an electrical discharge occurs, Swan devised the following original method. A shallow glass saucer containing a viscous resinous mixture was interposed in the spark-gap of a powerful induction coil. One spark terminal of the coil, shaped in the form of a ball, was suspended over the centre of the viscous surface, the other terminal being formed into a metallic casing to fit and support the glass saucer. When the ball was positively electrified, the viscous material was gathered up into a central heap under the ball. Immediately surrounding the heap was an annular space, from which streamed outwards branched rays puckering the surface into radial ridges and furrows. When the ball was negatively charged, a central dimple or depression was formed, surrounded by an annulus of rays of shorter and less vigorous character.

By using a solid cake of resin or shellac instead of the viscous mixture, and subjecting this to an electrical discharge, and subsequently dusting the surface with sulphur powder or lycopodium to bring out the positive stress figure, and red lead to bring out the negative effect, Swan was able to obtain graphic records of these electrical stresses in a durable form, affording a very simple and beautiful means of studying the different electrical effects of positive and negative discharge.

These experiments were shown to Lord Armstrong, who was himself engaged upon similar researches, and many of the stress figures so obtained were used by him to illustrate his monograph on *Electric Movement in Air and Water*, published in 1894.

As the result of these experiments it was found that, to obtain a coil that would be permanent in its working powers, it was necessary to use dielectric media which, amongst other necessary characteristics, showed no tendency to move under electrical strain.

The possibility of finding some improved means of producing electricity electro-chemically was another problem to which Swan devoted a good deal of time and thought at this period. His idea was to make an electrolytic cell in which the electrolyte would be imperishable and need no renewal, and in which an oxidizable gas, such as carbon monoxide or hydrogen, would be supplied to and oxidized in the electrolyte, air or oxygen being supplied to sustain the oxidizing power of the electrolyte. He was encouraged in following up this idea by a successful preliminary experiment. Taking a diaphragm of thin Berlin porcelain " biscuit," he had lightly silvered both sides, and then dipped it in a solution of caustic soda so that the porcelain soaked up and became saturated with the caustic soda. The diaphragm, after drying, was then so arranged that oxygen could be supplied to one side and hydrogen to the other, whilst it was heated to a temperature well above the melting-point of sodium hydroxide. Under these conditions it was found that an electromotive force of over one volt was sustained between the two faces of the diaphragm.

Although no practically useful gas-cell resulted from these researches, nevertheless they afford an interesting and typical example of the methodical, painstaking, and persistent way in which Swan attacked a problem of this character.

To achieve his object it was necessary to find a metal which could be made sufficiently porous to be permeable to the gases to be used, but impermeable to the leakage of the fused alkaline electrolyte, a metal which also was capable of delivering the gas to the electrolyte in an ionized condition. It was necessary to find a suitable non-conducting refractory material for containing the fused alkali. It was necessary, further, to find metallic oxides unattacked by the fused alkali and capable of acting as depolarizers in such a cell.

All these matters involved lengthy researches, which Swan pursued with exhaustive and unflagging patience, leaving untried nothing which his great range of knowledge of the properties of materials could suggest as likely to succeed.

Besides possessing this wide technical knowledge, he also possessed a high degree of skill and ingenuity in devising apparatus for his experiments. He was extremely resourceful in improvising apparatus from the simplest and most ordinary materials. Yet, although so simply put together, it was always neat and apt for its purpose ; there was nothing slovenly or slipshod about it. Dexterous and careful in his own manipulative methods, he insisted upon care and correctness on the part of those who assisted him. To take the simplest illustration : if a hole had to be bored in a cork, it must be done properly. Clumsiness or a " botched " job could not be tolerated. The borer had first to be well and truly sharpened, the cork carefully selected ; the borer slightly lubricated so

I

that it did not drag the cork, and finally applied with a carefully regulated screwing pressure. Similarly, in soldering and such-like simple laboratory operations there was a prescribed routine from which no deviation was permitted.

Though his hands were large, his manipulation was extremely delicate and deft, and he thoroughly enjoyed demonstrating to the novice or inexpert how the thing *should* be done.

In conducting his experiments his eye and mind were always alert to detect some unlooked-for result. Even in an exasperating failure he was ready to see some point of interest. Writing to one of his daughters at this time, he says :—

" The laboratory is claiming much of my spare time and the results of my work there lead to much air-castle building, which form of architecture may or may not materialize. One of my latest results has been the accidental production of a large crop of microscopic crystals, which, when agitated in the water through which they are diffused, cause twirling wreaths of white satin to wind about the beaker; and when at rest, they settle to the bottom, making a pearl-white covering so exactly like frosted silver that if they had been first produced in the days of alchemy instead of these degenerate days, when the reality of everything is doubted, even to matter itself, their production would have opened up to the happy discoverer bright dreams of wealth and immortality. As it is, I look upon it as a very pretty experiment, and at the same time a most temper-provoking failure ; but the chemist has to bear so many such failures that he is impervious to their effect, and without remorse he empties the shining gems down the sink. But I have kept a few for you to see."

The presidency of scientific societies involved inaugural addresses, lectures, and other public speaking. Upon the composition of these addresses and speeches he bestowed infinite pains, fastidiously altering and amending up to the last moment wherever a passage seemed capable of happier phrasing. This scrupulous desire for the *mot juste*, commendable enough in considered composition, made Swan somewhat halting as an impromptu speaker. He would often keep his hearers waiting an apparently unreasonable length of time, rather than use a word which he felt did not fully convey the meaning he intended.

In 1898 he chose, as the topic of his Presidential Address to the Institution of Electrical Engineers, the rise and progress of electro-chemical industries, referring more particularly to the use and possibilities of the electric furnace, as, for example, in aluminium manufacture, and pointing out to the young electrical engineer the desirability of adding to his normal technical equipment a competent knowledge of the principles of electro-chemical practice, as the means of making broader and surer his pathway to success. During the term of his office the Institution suffered the loss of two of its members, pre-eminent in the electrical world for their scientific achievements, to whose death he referred in the following words : " But, gentlemen, while I have been speaking of the progress of the Institution and of its gains, I have also been thinking of its losses. I have been thinking of the death of Latimer Clark and of that other loss, that climax of tragedy, the haunting memory of which follows us even here—the death of John Hopkinson. Latimer Clark died in the serene maturity of his 76 years, honoured and loved of all men—after many a gallant and successful fight to compel the forces of Nature into a profitable alliance, and to wrest from her obstinate keeping the keys of knowledge. Latimer Clark was one of the foremost of that band of great English engineers to whom we owe, and to whom the world owes, the all-embracing boon of ocean-telegraphy. To him we are also indebted for many valuable contributions to those ideas and methods of exact measurement of that intangible thing we call electricity, one of the outcomes of which is the Board of Trade Unit.

" With Dr. Hopkinson, the case is widely different. For him, the future seemed as full of promise as the past was of achievement. But little more than half the full measure of man's life had been spent. While the distaff was yet full, 'came the blind Fury with the abhorrèd shears, and slit the thin-spun life.'

" In the problems which confront us, we shall often miss his wise counsel. This is not the time nor the place for speaking of the great attainments of John Hopkinson, but there is one thing which I feel you will allow me to allude to, and that is his sturdy patriotism.

" At a time when the clouds of war hung threateningly over us, Dr. Hopkinson proposed and carried out the organization of a corps of Electrical Engineer Volunteers. His idea was that it would be a prudent and wise employment of valuable raw material, to utilize the special knowledge of the electrical engineer to assist in the defence of the country, and help to make it strong and safe against possible encroachment or aggression. He held the faith, which we also hold, that the welfare of the world is bound up with the welfare of Britain. If that faith be true, patriotism and philanthropy are one, and to employ the resources of science in the defence of our rights, and in the maintenance of our power, is a sacred duty, owed not only to ourselves but to mankind."

It should be recorded that Swan proposed for membership of the Institution of Electrical Engineers the first lady member, Mrs. Hertha Ayrton, the wife of the distinguished electrician, Professor Ayrton, and herself distinguished in science, more particularly in connection with the study of the electric arc light. She was elected, and for long continued to hold the unique position of being the sole lady member of the Institution.

Upon his retirement from the presidency, Swan was made an honorary member of the Institution—the highest distinction which that body can confer.

His addresses and lectures to learned societies contain for the most part matter merely of technical or contemporary interest. But here and there occur passages which reflect Swan's views on questions of more general and permanent concern. In a popular lecture delivered in January 1903, at the Durham College of Science, and later at the Literary and Philosophical Society in Newcastle, on " Fire and Light," he takes occasion to draw attention to a subject which he always regarded as one of vital national importance, namely, the urgent necessity for economy in the use of our coal supplies.

" Doubtless the coal deposits of the world are incalculably great, yet we know that in our own island they are limited and are a rapidly diminishing quantity. That consideration admonishes us to copy the thrift of Nature, and to apply the principles of science to help in the husbanding of our store.

" Commerce and industry exact from us the yearly tribute of more than two hundred million tons of our national patrimony. Supposing we are economically right in fully responding to their demands, yet it is not only a measure of prudence, it is a patriotic duty to avail ourselves of every means of assistance that science can give, towards reducing, so far as it can be reduced without detriment to those interests, the sum of this tremendous payment. That we are neglecting this duty the pall of smoke that overhangs our manufacturing towns is proof positive ! That ' blanket of the dark ' is the sign of reckless waste, which in its effects is destructive of natural beauty, of decent living, and of life itself. Science offers remedies ; if they are not radical and complete, they at least provide means of amelioration. Science offers a strong helping hand toward the mitigation of this cause of moral and physical deterioration and national loss. It is no exaggeration to say that we can get all, and more than all the heat we require for our houses, and all the power we require for working our machinery, with half the present consumption of coal, and with less than half the smoke we now make. The means of effecting the almost total abolition of coal smoke are well known, and are largely within practical reach; and gas and electricity can mutually assist in contributing towards the accomplishment of this desirable end.

" The moral of my story is this : Let us use the benefactions of Nature carefully ; and let us apply all the resources of science to the economization of coal."

The need for improved and more widespread education in science, as the basis of this country's industrial prosperity, was another theme upon which he held decided and outspoken views.

In his address to the students of the School of Pharmacy in October 1903, after contrasting the opportunities for learning available when he first " smelt powder—powder in the form of aloes, gamboge and scammony, and other nauseous drugs"—with those accessible to students of the present day, he goes on to emphasize the need for still further national progress in the apprehension and use of the resources of science.

" There is, no doubt, a considerable change for the better, but it did not come till long after it was an urgent necessity, and it has not yet gone nearly far enough. We see one of the evil consequences of our educational deficiencies in the much less rapid progress that we, as a nation, have made, comparatively with our industrial rivals, more especially in those branches of industry which are the outcome of the scientific discoveries of recent times, and which largely depend for their evolution and successful practical application on original research and on the intelligent appreciation, by the capitalist and commercial class, of the resources of science and the advantages of high scientific training and scientific work as auxiliary forces in promoting industrial development and progress.

" We are still desperately in need of more thorough general education and of the means of larger and better organized exploration of new fields of knowledge. While we are slowly learning by the painful process of ruinous loss the lesson of our want in this respect, our competitors abroad have long been reaping the benefits of their earlier recognition of the value of knowledge and of the means of acquiring knowledge as a basis of industrial prosperity."

He then goes on to speak of the distractions of pleasure and sport.

" Here, you are placed in circumstances which make learning comparatively easy. The atmosphere is the atmosphere of study, you are in a marching corps, and you must keep step ; the contact-action principle comes into play ; the total effect is that you are helped in the assimilation of knowledge, and in the formation of good habits of work.

" It is not to be denied that even in the best circumstances the routine grind of study is often in conflict with natural and healthy impulses towards other uses of time and thought, and that it requires a not inconsiderable amount of restraint and self-denial to do full justice to the main business you have set yourselves to accomplish. I strongly sympathize with you in the inevitable struggle you will often have to make in choosing the line of duty rather than the line of pleasure.

" I do not counsel such austerity as would deprive you of any and every pleasure ; but, knowing how strong and how many are the temptations to the profitless expenditure of time, and that the London student is not, as a rule, prone to excessive devotion to study, or excessive aversion from amusement, I do not feel that the danger is great of any serious harm in the direction of excessive abstinence. By all means take athletic exercise, as much as is necessary for your health, and do not deny yourself pleasure or amusement in moderation; but do not let indulgence interfere with work.

" Your special duty, as students, is study. Be earnest, be whole-hearted in your work—find your pleasure in it. If you look at it in the right way, you will have no

difficulty in discovering that your work, or some section
of your work, contains within itself the elements of refined
pleasure, the means of recreative enjoyment and delightful pastime.

" The particular studies that you are now either entering on, or in the midst of, are of a kind to give exercise to
all your previous knowledge, and to develop some faculties
not much cultivated in ordinary elementary education,
more especially the faculty of observation—such observation, I mean, as your lessons in botany and chemistry will
give occasion for, and which, whatever the immediate use
you may make of the knowledge they impart, will prove
an intellectual possession of inestimable and life-long
advantage.   They will give you interests and pleasures
that wealth cannot give—a wider outlook and more intimate acquaintance with Nature, that best of all acquaintances, the most inexhaustible in variety and charm, the
most reticent and inscrutable, and yet the best worth
questioning and communing with."

In advocating the taking up of hobbies as an added
interest in their work, he instances cases of distinguished
chemists among his friends : Henry Brady and Barnard
Proctor, who had found pleasure within the compass of
the student's work—Brady in microscopic research in a
branch of natural history which gave him high rank as
a man of science, and afforded a source of infinite delight
and an unfailing solace in failing health; and Proctor, also
an ardent naturalist and author of a work on Practical
Pharmacy, which is a monument to his technical knowledge and ingenuity.

Swan's lectures and addresses at times reveal also the
reflective and philosophical side of his mind.

Speaking in Newcastle on " Modern Developments of
Photography," he turns in conclusion from the marvels
of Science to contemplate and compare the surpassing
wonders of Nature.

The lecture ended with these words :

" In a little while these marvellous things of which I

have been speaking will pass into the region of the commonplace and become part and parcel of ordinary experience. But we shall still look forward with expectancy to the achievements of science in the future, and go on striving with infinite effort to lift some corner of the veil that shrouds the darkness of the unknown. It is impossible to repress those longings and those strivings for newer knowledge ; but, after all, we shall find nothing in the *new* more inherently wonderful than in the *old* ; nothing more wonderful, and nothing more beautiful than the light of the sun as it bursts in the glory of a new day upon an English landscape in springtime—

' Kissing with golden face the meadows green,
Gilding pale streams with heavenly alchemy.' "

In October 1901 the University of Durham, which had already given him the degree of M.A. *honoris causa,* also conferred upon him the honorary degree of D.Sc.

In 1902 the Royal Photographic Society awarded him the Progress Medal for the invention of the Autotype Process.[1] The medal of the Society of Chemical Industry was given him in 1903 "for conspicuous service in applied chemistry." In December 1904 the Royal Society awarded him the Hughes Medal "for his invention of the incandescent electric lamp and his other inventions and improvements in the practical applications of electricity." The President, Sir William Huggins, in presenting the medal at the Royal Society's dinner, mentioned, though not as directly included in the award, "his inventions in dry-plate photography, which had so much increased our powers of experimental investigation."

In returning thanks, Swan drew attention to the fact that of the eight medals, annually awarded by the Royal Society, seven had, on this occasion, been given for discovery and one for invention. He went on to speak of the attributes of an inventor as follows :

[1] The carbon process, see Chapter III.

" An inventor is an opportunist, one who takes occasion by the hand ; who, having seen where some want exists, successfully applies the right means to attain the desired end. The means may be largely, or even wholly, something already known, or there may be a certain originality or discovery in the means employed. But in every case the inventor uses the work of others. If I may use a metaphor, I should liken him to the man who essays the conquest of some virgin alp. At the outset he uses the beaten track, and, as he progresses in the ascent, he uses the steps made by those who have preceded him, wherever they lead in the right direction; and it is only after the last footprints have died out that he takes ice-axe in hand and cuts the remaining steps, few or many, that lift him to the crowning height which is his goal."

The description is typical, for it illustrated the modesty and generous acknowledgment of the work of others which characterized any reference he ever made to his own work.   Contentious claims and jealousies in scientific matters were to him utterly abhorrent.   Ever ready to applaud merit in others, he could never bear to claim it for himself.

The honour of knighthood was conferred upon him in November 1904.   During the same year he acted as a member of the Royal Commission for the St. Louis Exhibition.

On July 8th, 1905, after giving an address on the progress of electrical engineering on the occasion of Degree Day at the University of Liverpool, he formally opened the new electro-technical laboratories.

In 1906 the Prince of Wales, as President of the Society of Arts, presented him with the Albert Medal for his " inventions in connection with the electric lamp and with photography."

During the latter years of his residence in London, besides all the work connected with his different offices and businesses, he had heavy financial anxiety through having to pay large sums of money on behalf of a friend, who had been a help to him in earlier days and for whom he had given a guarantee to a bank. Though the amount involved was very much greater than had been anticipated when the guarantee was given, it was finally met. The inroad which this liability made into the fortune which he had won for his family was a subject of great concern to him, and the worry consequent upon these transactions told upon his strength, already overtaxed with the labours of a long life.

He was no longer equal to the strain of the many calls which life in London made upon him. The time had come " to take in sail."

CHAPTER X

A VERY imperfect picture of Swan would be presented, unless to the account already given of his experimental work and business activities there were added some glimpses of his social and domestic environment. Outstanding in this aspect of his life was the never-failing boon of his wife's sympathetic companionship, revealed best perhaps through the medium of the letters that passed daily between them, whenever separated at home or abroad. Something, too, should be said of his affectionate relations with all his children and of the close interest he showed in their various occupations and hobbies. This, too, appears in the numerous letters by which he kept any absent member of the family informed of the happenings at home; telling usually of some special episode or incident with a graphic touch and particularity of detail surprising in one apparently so abstracted and contemplative.

Although the removal to London had been made chiefly for greater convenience in attending scientific and company meetings, it incidentally gave rise to more numerous social engagements. There was much entertaining in the scientific circle in which Swan found most of his friends; and he and his wife did their share of it with zest.

The visitors' book, begun at "Lauriston" in 1884 and ended at Warlingham in 1914, besides being a collection of names which any autograph hunter might well covet, shows a record of abundant hospitality and of a wide circle of friends. Looking at random through its pages, one lights upon names which recall memorable personalities. To mention only a few of the more intimate friends, there is W. Holman-Hunt, that faithful artist and delightful raconteur; Dinah Craik, who wrote *John Halifax, Gentleman* in her youth—a book "all about love" says

Mrs. Carlyle, cynically prophesying, " God help her !
She'll sing to another tune if she go on living and writing
for twenty years "; a prediction which Mrs. Craik's serene
and benevolent aspect in old age sufficiently refuted ; Sir
Hubert von Herkomer, most versatile of modern artists ;
Professor John Perry, the warm-hearted and pugnacious
Irish mathematician, who loved to trail some fantastic
theory to entice his hearers into a wordy contest ; Pro-
fessor and Mrs. Ayrton, notable electricians both ; Sir
William and Lady Huggins, lured with difficulty from
their contemplation of the heavenly bodies ; Sir William
and Lady Crookes, he a practical man of science and a
mystic, and she, most kindly and downright of sensible
women ; Sir Oliver Lodge, Sir William Barrett and
Professor Myers—a trinity of psychical researchers ; Sir
William Ramsay, Professor John Hopkinson, Sir Edward
Frankland, Professor Silvanus Thompson, Sir Benjamin
Baker, and Professor Hughes. These few names, for they
are but a few taken at random from a multitude, will
perhaps suffice to convey some idea of the interesting and
delightful circle within which as guest, or more happily
as host, Swan enjoyed the society of his friends.

Besides the exchanges of hospitality and other social
diversions which life in London afforded, there were
summer visits to the seaside and occasional trips to the
Continent.

For many years the north-east coast was chosen for
the summer holidays. Alnmouth, with its attractions of
river, sea and golf links, was the favourite place. Here
Swan for the first time took up golf, and, though past the
age of three-score years and ten, he showed considerable
aptitude, and derived great enjoyment from the game;
particularly when, on one memorable occasion, with a
well-hit cleek-shot, he did the first hole, a short one,
in one.

One summer was spent at Dunbar, and another at
Whitby, where Swan had the pleasure of making the
acquaintance of James Russell Lowell, for whose poetry,

particularly the poem of *The Vision of Sir Launfal,* he had a great admiration.

One year the keep of Bamburgh Castle was rented. Its historical and romantic associations from Saxon times to the Jacobite rising of 1715, and its noble situation overlooking the " long strand of Northumberland " and the Farnes and Holy Island, with their memories of early saints, appealed to all ; while to live in a four-square fortress with a reputed ghost in the night-nursery, and an equally well-authenticated witch sitting in the form of a toad at the bottom of the castle well, was a notable experience. However, the only occasion for psychical research was when Swan was called upon to investigate a ghostly wail which had disturbed his wife at night. The uncanny sound was ultimately traced to a curled piece of paper in the chimney of her room that acted as a trumpet when the wind blew.

Another year a charming house near Dolgelly was taken, where the river and mountains attracted the younger members of the family, whilst Swan, content with a more distant view of the landscape, added sketching in pastels to his other amusements.

The Christmas holidays were usually spent at home ; but in 1900 and 1901 Swan went with several members of his family to spend the winter at Caux, in Switzerland, where he entered with zest into the less strenuous forms of winter sport—lugeing and curling.

Such, in brief, was the scheme of the family life at this time. It is, however, through the medium of his letters that one gets the best insight into the more intimate traits of Swan's mind and character.

He lets himself go in his letters ; there is nothing formal or stereotyped in them. Indeed, he writes with a greater spontaneity and *naïveté* than he was wont to show in ordinary conversation. Whatever the topic, his letters are never dull. He had the alchemist's art of transmuting dross to gold—through the medium of imagination. So, by original and picturesque turns of phrase and expression, he could give freshness and piquancy even to what might, with other telling, seem trivial and commonplace.

He writes from Holland Park to his wife on the Riviera:

" I have just returned from the ' dim rich city,' very dreary and dim to-day, with rain and drizzle and no sunshine. I had a hansom both in and out, which was better than if I had gone by the underground railway. I was, in fact, at the very door of the Mansion House Station on my way home ' when a beautiful chariot there came ' in the shape of a spick and span brand-new hansom, leather lined, with dainty horse and trappings, smart man with cape and rakish hat. I could not resist it, and so, instead of taking the easy *descent* to the lower regions, I climbed up and had the reward of virtue in purer air and the music of the bells as we clattered along. I told the man how he had won my heart. I was glad to find that the cab and horse were his own. I might have known that ; the horse was so well groomed."

To his daughter, M. E. S., who had gone to Capri to paint, March 12th, 1893, he writes :

" I need hardly say that I have followed your movements, as I could trace them through the letters from you that have been passed round, with the greatest interest, and with much rejoicing that you have had so many pleasant experiences and no misadventures. It seems as though the object of your visit to Italy will in some measure be realized. I trust you will come back refreshed both in mind and body. To that end, it seems to me, one thing especially is necessary, and that is that you should do your art work less laboriously, with less effort, for you really disable yourself by excess of effort. Do not attempt difficult things, and what you begin—finish. There are some hard rules for you. But I am sure you will not find them bad if you follow them. If you cannot do all you want, just do the best you can, but oh ! *do it easily*. You will do it far, far better.

Perfection is impossible—let it go, and just do the best you comfortably can.

"Are not orange and lemon trees *very very* difficult to paint the souls of? I greatly fear so, and you don't want to paint them as otherwise than living. When you spoke of painting orange and lemon trees, I thought with heart-sinking of that wind-blown thorn at Bamburgh— a beautiful subject regarded poetically, but very, very hard to paint, so as to tell its pathetic story, and otherwise it was just a scraggy, haggard bush. Why am I talking so? Why, my dear girl, because I have so often felt the weakening effect of failure, or only partial success. It is too disheartening to make it safe or healthy to run the risk of it, much less to court it by too ambitious attempts! Only attempt what you can succeed in, and succeed in *easily*.

"Take your pleasure gladly, not sadly. Let the touches on your canvas be light ones, and as unconscious as possible. I mean, let them be inspirational, mediumistic, yourself being an almost passive instrument."

58 Holland Park,
May 23rd, 1896.

To M. E. S., in Majorca.

" I am hoping to go to Glasgow on or about the 14th of June to take part in the jubilee of the Professorship of Lord Kelvin. Yesterday H. M. sent two tickets for the Opera at Covent Garden. Isobel and I went. It was her first experience of opera, and she did enjoy it. The piece was *La Favorita*—not by a long way up to Wagner —'twas full of absurdities in fact, but with some sweet airs in it, and one or two dramatic scenes; and they were very well rendered.

" On Wednesday we ' took a wessel ' and went up the Thames. The 'wessel' was an electric launch yclept *The Lady Lena*. We went past Clieveden and Great Marlow and Hurley. We had luncheon on board in the most approved style in a beautiful backwater near

Hurley. The hawthorn blossom and the chestnut blossom and the overhanging willows and the buttercups among the grass, and the sunshine and the thunder showers—all contributed charm and delight to a day never to be forgotten. We heard the nightingale, and I saw both a kingfisher and a heron. It is only the second sight of the kingfisher that I have had; the first time was at Sunderland when I was a boy, 10 years old. I had always longed to see the blue flash again, and now I have seen it ! I left the party taking tea at ' The Compleat Angler ' at Great Marlow, and hurried back by train to dine at Sir David Salomons'. I have been awfully dissipated in that way—next night, Thursday, I was the guest of Dr. Frankland, who asked most particularly after you—the dear man he is ! The party was at the Athenæum, to meet the P. R. S. I sat next but one to Sir Joseph,[1] and had a good deal of interesting talk with him."

October 31st, 1897.

To M. W., acknowledging birthday greetings.

" Thank you, thank you, again and again, for your most precious thought of me to-day. If any power on earth has the magic in it to turn dross to gold, sour to sweet, surely it is the power of love—and it is wholly by the influence of this power and through a curious faculty that good people have for seeing in others the goodness that is in themselves alone, that I to-day have had so many loving words addressed to me and so many other tokens of regard that seemed to the givers to speak more clearly than words. I feel absolutely unworthy of all this outpouring of love, and have no words fit to acknowledge it, and no heart to refuse it either."

July 27th, 1898.

To H. S., at Plombières.

" Our American friend will, I expect, be gratified with the news of to-day that Spain is suing for peace. I

[1] Sir Joseph Lister, afterwards Lord Lister.

K

hope the news may prove true and that the war is at an end, and that America will demonstrate to the world that, as France once boasted of herself having the exceptional virtue of going to war ' for an idea,' so she too can make the same boast, and with better reason than France; for after making that declaration she took Savoy and Nice. If America comes out of this ordeal well and keeps to her promises of philanthropic motive in the war, she will acquire for herself, beyond all cavil, a patent of nobility among nations which none may gainsay."

Writing on June 21st, 1899, from Folkestone, where he had gone to convalesce after a short illness, to H. S. at Plombières, he says :

" We have had a delightful adventurous day. It was a very fine morning, and I had ordered a carriage. I told the driver to go ' deep into the country where the wild roses were thick on the hedges.' As we went along, the thought dawned that Canterbury was only 16 miles off, and then the question arose, why should we not drive there ? Not being able to find a good reason for not going, we went; and we have had an excursion to be treasured in the memory; but without any treasuring it is not at all likely to be lost.

" The country is truly delicious, and though we may be losing trade to the Germans and the Americans, yet I never saw the fields so palpably rejoice in the glory of their gay attire. The roses—there is a great bowl here that we ravished from their kindred—the roses have not in the least degenerated; they are just the same as they were when they first sent a thrill of pleasure through my boyish heart—my first and last flower love.

" We, of course, wished for you and Mary, for Mary especially, as we were passing a great field gorgeous with a mixture of poppy, rose-coloured vetch (the colour of bright coloured clover) and white campion. Truly you ' scarce could see the grass for flowers.' There was enough, but no more than enough green to fully complement the other colours and enrich the effect. We did long for you both to see the most splendid field I ever saw in my life!

"Hilda had not seen Canterbury, and I had almost forgotten the beautiful old city; so that we both had the pleasure of learning it. We went over a great part of the cathedral, and were duly impressed with its magnificence. We had a good luncheon at the Fountain Hotel, and set out at three to return. And we had strawberries and grapes on the way by way of dessert, real fresh country strawberries, the sweetest I have tasted for long. Oh, we only wanted you with us to have made our day perfect! I feel much better notwithstanding all the liberties taken in our Garden of Eden."

During the early part of 1900 most of the family were abroad, some in Switzerland, and Swan had escorted his wife from there to Rapallo, leaving her to spend a couple of months on the Riviera, while he returned to an England deep in the rigours of a dismal winter and the depression of the Boer War.

February 8th, 1900.

To H. S., at Rapallo.

"Here I am at my old desk in the familiar library, but not, alas! with the familiar figure in the opposite seat."

His wife's writing-table was a replica of his, and arranged so that he and she faced one another and could exchange papers and conversation across the joined tables. It was difficult to lure him to tackle the piled-up papers awaiting his attention on his writing-table; but, once there, he dealt with them in a masterly fashion.

"I have had a pretty busy day among my papers and in the laboratory, but I have not been quite up to work, for I feel the fatigue of travel even more to-day than I did yesterday. I feel the cold very much. It is horrible! Yet the sun has shone in the dull reluctant way that is its best behaviour in London."

February 11th, 1900.

" The newspapers to-day contain no good news.   It is evident that we have suffered another defeat.   I see Mr. Courtney has been making a speech against the war.   It is not possible to deny that he makes out a very good case against it.   There is a general sense of depression at the losses of every kind it has entailed."

February 20th, 1900.

To H. S., at Mentone.

" You will be sorry to hear that my dear old friend, Joe Cowen, is dead; his funeral takes place to-morrow, and I am going down to Newcastle this afternoon to attend it.   It is a great pain to me to think of another precious link with the past being broken, and it brings up to my mind the often-experienced thought and feeling of regret that I have not taken all the good out of these experiences that I might have done.

" Cowen was one of the friends of my youth; he helped me in my earliest electric light experiments by getting things made for me at his works that I wanted for my experiments, and he did this as a matter of pure friendship and kindness to me."

EXPRESS FROM NEWCASTLE,
February 22nd, 1900.

To H. S., at Mentone.

" I have finished my short visit to Newcastle and am now speeding home.

" We (John[1] and I) went together to Mr. Cowen's funeral—a painful ordeal but more painful still to have evaded it.   It involved the meeting with many old friends—friends of our youth—and the realization of how many have passed away.   The very countryside spoke pathetically of the past.   I had once known Blaydon and Ryton well.   Yesterday I felt like a stranger

---

[1] His brother, John Cameron Swan.

in a strange land, or, if not quite strange, with only shadowy recollections hanging about it. I saw the house where I visited Joseph Cowen 52 years ago. You will see from the paper I send how deeply the public sympathy was stirred on the occasion of the funeral."

March 1st, 1900.

" You will have had the good news of the Relief of Ladysmith at last. Here it has caused great popular rejoicing. Even at Notting Hill there is evidence, in the form of bunting. As I turn to look over the roof of my laboratory, I see quite a string of flags, the Union Jack conspicuous among them. Anything almost that would help to bring the war to an end, not dishonourable to us, would be most welcome, and I think this and the surrender of the 4000 with Cronje must tend in that direction.

" The girls and I went to see Benson's rendering of the *Midsummer Night's Dream* last night. It was most beautifully done, and I enjoyed it, as did all the girls; but I am sure we should have enjoyed it more if we had had the Ladysmith news to raise our spirits to a higher capacity of enjoyment. It is the first play that I have seen since the war.

" I am on the point of going out to a Royal Society meeting, chiefly with the object of seeing Sir Wm. Crookes there and dining with him afterwards."

March 3rd, 1900.

" I was at the Royal Institution lecture last evening. It was my first visit to the old place since I was on the Continent. The Duke of Northumberland was in the chair, wearing his star and ribbon. The lecture was on the relation of malarial fever to the mosquito, and disclosed a most important discovery likely to be a great boon to humanity in the way of preventing malarial fever."

March 4th, 1900.

" I told you in my last letter that I was going to the send-off dinner we have given to the active contingent of the Electrical Engineers Volunteers. It was a most interesting and altogether successful function. Out of a body of about 200 of the Electrical Volunteer Corps 50 have volunteered for active service and it was to these 50 that the dinner was given. I was one of the hosts and had a captain on each side, one Captain Brady of the R.E., adjutant to the E.E.V. Corps, on my left, and Captain Henry M. Leaf of the E.E.V. Corps on my right. I found both my neighbours very pleasant, Captain Leaf particularly interesting. Lord Kelvin was, as Honorary Colonel to the Corps, in the presidential chair, and made several most admirable speeches. In one, and the most eloquent, of these he held up to admiration the extraordinary manifestation of magnanimous self-sacrificing patriotism which this war had developed and of which the volunteering for active service of the contingent of 50 of our electrical engineers was a fine example. For, as he said, every one of those men was voluntarily leaving home and business prospects and business occupations of profit, to enter upon a life of toil and hardship and danger, offering their all, even to their very lives, for the sake of the honour of the Empire and the defence of the principles of freedom and right.

" Major Crompton also spoke, and spoke very well, going into detail of the preparation made for the work of the E.E.V. and what that work would consist of. He is not going out with this first contingent, but may possibly go out if a second contingent should be sent for. The principal duty will be the management of searchlight apparatus which has been specially invented for the occasion ; also the field telephone, the line being laid with the help of the bicycle. General Webber and Captain Lloyd of the R.E. (who is going out as chief officer of the contingent) and our good friend, Professor

Perry, all made excellent speeches. There was also diversion in the form of song and recitation, both good ; and, as you may imagine, boundless enthusiasm. There were several ' jolly good fellows,' and many had cheers given in their honour. It was an occasion to lift one's hopes and aspirations, though nominally ' a dinner.' Lord Kelvin asked after you, dear genial man ! "

March 5th, 1900.

To H. S., at Cannes.

" It is still bitterly cold, but altho' the temperature and dullness suggest winter, there are a few signs of irrepressible spring in the crocus blossoms which are just being discovered by the sparrows. They have ' come before the swallows dare,' but not before the sparrows. They are gathering spring flowers to their hearts' content. Even the bushes are tired of long waiting, and are looking out inquiringly through the green eyes of their buds. But I assure you it is bitter cold, and you are very well where you are."

March 7th, 1900.

" Here it is as wintry as ever, but that is nothing new for us; as some one (Walpole, I think) said, ' Spring has set in with its usual severity,' and at this moment I am cowering over the fire with the writing-board on my knee.

" Is it not very nice of the Queen to stay in London during this anxious time ? It seems to show that she cannot enjoy things selfishly while her people are in need of all the sympathy and encouragement she can give them."

March 10th.

" The City has been much delighted with the Queen's visit, and has shown its pleasure by crowds and much vociferation—also by a lavish display of bunting. Everybody seems to be delighted with the occasion, and it is truly a relief from the dullness and depression that has been prevailing."

March 12th, 1900.

" But what of your own birthday ? Our good wishes—or rather the formal expression of them— cannot reach you in the wonted way, early in the morning; and wireless telegraphy is not yet developed far enough to circumvent the difficulty, except that I am sure you will, through an older kind of wireless telegraphy, by sympathy or thought transference, by the subtle power that binds heart to heart, know full well that we are thanking God for your past, and entreating blessings for the future."

March 19th, 1900.

" I have had a good long walk in the Park. The cold continues as pinching as ever. There has been a fall of snow during the night, and as one passed along the streets one saw it raked into heaps at the sides, and in the shaded patches of the Park the snow still lay unmelted. But though it is cold, the wind is less, and the sun occasionally shines in a bleary way. I am glad you have the good fortune to be where it is warm and where sweet-scented flowers grow. Thank you for material evidence of that. The violets scented the room when I unfolded my letter, and the sprig of wallflower was delightful to behold. Cold as it is, the crocus makes a bold brave show, both before and behind our house."

CHAPTER XI

HOLIDAYS

THE summer holidays of that year, 1900, were spent in Cornwall, and he produced some charming little pictures in pastel—though he felt the medium a fumbling one, in spite of its technique presenting fewer difficulties to an amateur than either water-colour or oil-painting.

In September he went with his two younger sons, Kenneth and Percival, to the Paris Exhibition.

EXHIBITION,

September 17th, 1900.

" I have just finished a long and rather toilsome promenade of the French exhibit of chemicals, and I am greatly impressed with the industry and skill and enterprise of the French in consequence; for the exhibit is truly a magnificent one."

HOTEL DE LILLE ET D'ALBION.

" The days are passing very quickly. The many useful and even wonderful things that are to be seen quite give one a sense of despair of any success in attempting to retain any mental record of them or of even a small proportion of them.

" This morning I attended the meeting of the Iron and Steel Institute and heard, besides, a few sentences spoken from the printed address of the President, Sir Wm. Roberts Austen, the sentences chosen being the beginning and end of the address, and a most admirable extempore abstract of a paper on Crystallographic Analysis of Steel by John Stead—brother of Wm. Stead and partner of John Pattinson. I utilized the opportunity of obtaining from him more than a half promise that he would—in about 6 months—give the Society of Chemical Industry a paper on some cognate subject. He is a most charming fellow. He said, ' Don't ask me ; let me for a time feel the elation that I feel to-day, having got rid of a burden I have carried for two years; and now that I am rid of it, I feel like an angel with wings, and that I have the power to fly.' But, for all that, I cruelly pressed my suit and got a promise from him, or something very near a promise, to pay in six months. Isaac Lowthian Bell, dear old man (85 !), and as young-looking and erect as I am, was at the meeting, and going to the, to him, more particularly interesting of the exhibits. I saw him look at and get all particulars of the great gas engine, worked by blast-furnace gas and promising valuable economies in the form of cheap motive power, auxiliary to iron-making. I spoke to him and introduced Kenneth. I also spoke to Austen. I have seen the electric furnaces worked to-day, and a recording telephone—so that if you don't happen to be at the instrument when some one speaks to you, the message spoken is recorded automatically, and can be reproduced afterwards as in the phonograph."

HOTEL DE LILLE ET D'ALBION,
September 19th, 1900.

" To-day we have been most of the time in the Fine Art section; and although I found it very interesting, I found it exceedingly tiring, so that my strength was spent almost alone on that to-day.

" I did, in addition, see the wonderful Creusot exhibit, that of the firm where all the Boer guns, or most of them, were made—the ' Long Toms,' etc. It is a wonderful example of the extensive—the *immensely* extensive and complete organization of the engineering factory methods of our day—where one proprietor gives employment to tens of thousands of men, and produces not only a great variety of engineering products, but some of them of gigantic size; bridges, cannon, shot, engines, dynamos, and the metals from which these are all made. I have not seen the Krupp exhibit, but I expect it is something like the Creusot one in its scope and the scale of the work it represents. America is not behindhand in this kind of elaborate and widespread factory organization, as several exhibits representative of its great works show; and Germany also. Beside Krupps, England presents a sorry spectacle. Here and there you see something English; but one is struck by the fewness of English exhibits and the general want of ' go ' they indicate. If the light exists with us, it is hidden somewhere. I walked through the French department, devoted to the illustration of the educational and research work done by the Government in furtherance of scientific knowledge bearing on agriculture and its improvement."

The last letter in 1900 is to his wife, written on the journey to Newcastle, December 30th and 31st, where he went to attend the funeral of his old friend, Lord Armstrong. It ends :

" As usual, but perhaps with a more solemn feeling than ever before, at the closing of the year and the opening of a new year, I think of you and of the children, and fervently pray that God may bless you in the future as He has blessed you in the past.—Still five minutes to midnight! It is strange to be absent from you, yet I am with you! The new year! God bless you! Jan. 1st, 1901."

The early part of 1901 was spent at Mentone with his wife and eldest daughter, whom he left there on his return to London at the end of February. About this time he began to feel a pain in his chest on walking up-hill or on cold days. This was the first symptom of his heart trouble.

March 5th, 1901.

" I have not been out much to-day. The day has been very bleak and rainy. But I did go out to attend a committee meeting of the Royal Society on the Hughes Medal design. I was prevailed on by Sir Michael Foster to write the obituary notice of Dr. Pole.

" I am just debating the question whether I shall submit myself to a cross-examination at a Board of Trade enquiry. It is a ticklish ordeal, but I think I must do it."

At the annual meeting of the Society of Chemical Industry, held at Glasgow in July 1901, he delivered his presidential address on the electro-chemical industry.

On his return he writes, July 30th, 1901, to H. S., at Alnmouth:

" I have just returned from my day in the City. I called at the office of the Society of Chemical Industry and saw the Secretary and Editor—and am correcting proofs of the matter arising out of the Glasgow meeting. I found they thought everything had gone well. What a pleasure it is to me to be able to repair the little faults of speech in the reports as printed ! If only we could have such revision of all our acts, what an added happiness to life ! "

January 31st, 1902.

" I have had another busy day in the city, sitting at a board meeting for 5 hours. Then I came home and took Hilda to call on Miss Paget.[1] We had a charming visit with bright conversation, some delicious singing of Purcell's music, and a talk of old times and the personalities that have glorified the past within our memory and, to a limited extent, our knowledge. It was an interesting hour."

February 6th, 1902.

" I have just returned after a long day's work. First at the Edison & Swan office—then immediately to Burlington House, where I attended a committee of the Royal Society, and afterwards the meeting. It was a slightly exceptional meeting, inasmuch as there was a lecture with brilliant experiments by Crookes. The Prince of Wales was present and was admitted to membership. The Prince of Wales, Lord Kelvin and Lord Rayleigh spoke. Lord Salisbury was present. It was a brilliant demonstration of some new and very interesting facts, which brought into view and explained the ' radiant matter ' experiments, some of which you have seen."

[1] Daughter of Sir James Paget, the famous surgeon.

He writes from the Sussex Hotel, St Leonards, where he was recruiting after an attack of influenza:

March 9th, 1902.

" This is Sunday, and a most delightful day it has been —warm and bright. At 10.30 we took a landau and drove to Battle—a delightful drive, through pleasant lanes— with singing birds all about—the lark prominent in the chorus. Then, in passing a wood with a wide-open gate, I went in among the budding saplings and crisp brown leaves, in search of a primrose, and I had at last the great pleasure of finding the treasure I enclose—the welcome token of spring."

The winter of 1902–3 was spent at Sandgate, and that of 1903–4 at Parkstone, near Bournemouth.

He often found the train a stimulus to letter-writing. Here are two typical specimens of his train letters:

On the line past Box Hill,
April 20th, 1904.

To H. S., at Bath.

" The journey promises to be delightful. The outlook on the green, daisy-garnished fields and fast-robing trees is wonderful in its hopeful beauty, and the temperature delicious in its languorous and dreamy ease. No doubt the ploughman with his steaming team would tell a different tale. We have just passed through the long tunnel and come out on a pastoral country now suffused with the haze of heat. Kingcups and primroses give us a golden borderland. Oh! what a miracle of the spring-kindled energy of life the single week has wrought! We must see as much of it as possible when I return from the dim city. Blackthorn, full of blossom! All trees, besides, either green or budding in almost flower-like richness of colour. Now we are passing Swindon; now Didcot Junction. The country between, on a day and at a season like this, is enough to make any man born in it and of it proudly patriotic. Goring! with Clieveden woods hanging lovingly on Thames-side. There will be the kingfisher there ! Pangbourne—a charming reach of the river with many boats and a pair of oars and happy lovers —one rowing and one steering in each—and groups of children, happy too they must be, gathering cowslips in the bright bordering meadows.

" Reading and smoke ! But it is soon past and the memory of it washed out by glorious gorse-bushes all a-flower on the railway banks.

" Maidenhead ! We cross the Thames once more. We are nearing London and prose. Fairyland is left behind ; it embraces Bath and the country between, and doubtless beyond. But not even London can quite shut out the spring sunshine to-day. Here is the most whitely-blossoming orchard I have seen this year ! Acton ! Paddington (4.38)."

ON THE LINE JUST PAST SELBY,
July 9th, 1906.

To H. S.

" Newspapers so far have been my sole companions, and they afford much occupation for the eyes and not a little for the mind. There are many things reported in them in the nature of news, and written by way of comment, which raise many questions and afford ample speculative material for all the leisure of the long journey I have before me. And as you know I never felt the time hang heavily on my hands while passing through the green country on a summer's day like this. How glad I am to think you and Dorothy are enjoying that pleasure also. We have had sunshine nearly all the way, and the fields look their best, with the hay being gathered in and the grain upstanding in lusty youth and the promise of early ripeness. I could not but connect the picture that spread around me—miles on miles, telling of the labour of the husbandman, and not labour only, but highly trained and intelligent art—with the weedy patch of uncultivated land we lately saw at Rothamsted.[1] I do not know why the great industrial art of the agriculturist,

[1] An experimental patch.

the cultivation of the soil, should be so commonly looked down upon as an especially mean kind of labour ; for certainly, as a whole, it demands not only industry but skill and intelligence ; and it is wonderful how nearly rule-of-thumb practice in farming by the more intelligent and successful farmers has coincided with the principles evolved and inculcated by modern science. If I were speaking to a company of farmers, I should take off my hat and feel in how many things I was beholden to them, in how many ways they were my masters. The farmer is the most indispensable element of the social structure; I doubt if he is esteemed in proportion to his value in this respect. . . .

" Now we are abreast of the Cleveland Hills—past Thirsk—wild roses in plenty here—no, not in plenty, but in great abundance !

" Durham ! Glorious in the mellow light of a fair sunset ! Now is the time for a Turner ! We go right on without a moment's stop to drink in the beauty of it. The most precious things are the most neglected ! Ravensworth ! Low Fell ! The Tyne with its new bridge which must not be crossed till after to-morrow, when the King has proved that it is safe enough to bear his subjects. The old Castle and the New ! A very good journey ! "

Shipcote, Gateshead,
July 10*th*, 1904.

" I follow up my telegram of last night by reporting my arrival at Shipcote[1] near 11.15—the train was near half an hour late.

" It went by way of Sunderland, which added an unexpected interest to the journey for me—for it allowed me a glimpse of the old river and the bridge and places I knew when I was a boy, dreaming unfulfilled dreams of the future."

To his daughter, M. E. S., describing a dinner-party at the Holman-Hunts, he writes :

[1] The home of his brother-in-law, John Pattinson.

June 1906.

" We were a very small and homely party. Only Sir George Reid and Lady Reid and another lady being of the number, besides our host and hostess and ourselves. Holman was, as usual, full of anecdote and very entertaining—he is quite as good a story-teller as a painter. He told how the Battle of Waterloo was won not by Bill Adams, but by Wellington's good strategy, as graphically reported to him by an eye-witness, who was at Wellington's side during the battle. He also spoke of some of the details of Wolseley's night march before the Battle of Tel-el-Kebir in an interesting way. These battle scenes drew me on to speak of Shakespeare's wonderful picture of the two camps before Agincourt as told by way of prologue to Act V. of *Henry V.*, and to outrage all the decencies by reciting it. Was not that shocking bad taste ? "

January 20th, 1907.

To D. S.

" Kenneth and I went to the Royal Institution on Friday to hear Sir Andrew Noble lecture on 50 years' progress in explosives. He gave an astonishing account of the endless experiments made by himself in elucidation of the peculiar properties of the many different kinds of explosive these last 50 fruitful years have produced, and these showed that in regard to ' villainous saltpetre ' we of the British Empire are in no respect behind our bellicose neighbours. I am still pegging away in my laboratory in the endeavour to find an adequate reply to our continental rivals in the peaceful strife of electric lighting, and the discovery of the best and most economical lamp. I am finding, not for the first time, how slow are the paces of scientific progress."

May 30th, 1907.

To D. S.

" Mary will have told you of our motoring over the hill roads of Wales—we went over 250 miles in two days, or rather in three half days, and I think we passed through some of the most magnificent scenery in the island. At Port Madoc, and on the way to it, there was some of the most memorable, equally beyond description in words or on canvas. There is absolutely no vehicle for the translation of the impression made on one mind to the mind of another, nor is it at all possible for the most receptive mind, seeing what we saw, to take it all in. I can only hope that dim glimpses of the glory of it may sometimes in a happy moment revive and bless it.

" Motoring is a delightful mode of travel, but at 35 miles an hour it is to me a ' fearful joy ' ; but that pace was an exception, and I did thoroughly enjoy 18 to 20 miles an hour on the smooth straight, and for the most part empty, roads of the Welsh hills. The *exhilaration* of it is beyond words."

During the winter of 1908 Sir Joseph and Lady Swan went to Egypt—an adventurous journey at their time of life. One of the chief inducements to their going was to see their son, Percival, who was in the Public Works Department of the Egyptian service. Their daughter Isobel and her husband, Reginald Morcom, also went out that year and were with them on their journey to Luxor.

In a letter written to M. E. S. from the Winter Palace Hotel, Luxor, on January 3rd, 1908, Swan writes :

" I have just returned from a stroll around the outskirts of the great temple here—it was just after sunset, and I saw things in a half light and found them wonderfully picturesque. The contrast of the wretched slums that environ this immense monument of human power and human vanity was prodigious. The great colonnades, splendid in size and form, elaborately sculptured walls, covered with boastful historic story, jostled and were half buried in the dust-heaps of the most squalid hovels I ever saw used as the dwelling-places of humanity at its lowest depths of degradation. But then you know I have not been a great traveller, and there may be even worse conditions of living than this; but I have never seen them. The

L

gutter children of London wallow in mud—not very deep.
Here the almost naked urchins wallow in dust many
inches deep—dust that has been lived amongst for cen-
turies.   It is wonderful how they live under such adverse
conditions.   They not only live, but they seem in their
way to enjoy life and to be disposed to be merry over it
all.   It is surprising to find how many of the natives speak
English—even the babies speak it to some extent.   As I
passed through the slum I spoke of, behind the ruins of the
temple, two small children, the youngest not more than
3 or 4, spoke to me.   The baby said, ' Good evening,
Babba' (Father).   It was an unexpected greeting, and I
really don't think the motive was backsheesh.   I felt in
my pocket for a small coin and felt sorry not to find one.
So I only paid them back in their own coin."

Luxor,
January 5th, 1908.

" This morning we were up betimes and out to welcome
R. and I. on their arrival by the Nile steamer.   They
readily entered into the project we put before them to
make an excursion to Karnak and beg the help of M. le
Grain, the director of the excavations and restorations
there, which on our first visit he had promised.   This
project we carried into effect with great success, reaping a
very ample reward for a long and heavy tramp among the
debris of excavation work which we found in full operation.   M. le Grain has been engaged for twelve years in
unearthing and piecing together and erecting in their
original positions the tumbled and broken masses of the
most extensive and beautiful temple ruins to be found
anywhere in Egypt or in the world.   The area of the site
is enormous ; it is about equal to that of Pompeii.   The
walls and columns are covered with historic sculpture and
hieroglyphics of infinite interest to the Egyptologist and
historian, and even the uninitiated cannot but be moved
to wonder and inquiry by these books of stones.   There
is a magnificently polished and inscribed red granite

obelisk, far finer than the Luxor obelisk or Cleopatra's Needle. I do not believe that we shall ever see anything finer in the way of architectural ruins than those we have seen to-day. The process of re-erecting the fallen columns was shown to us in operation ; we also saw the swarm of half-naked black children—mites of 10 to 14 perhaps—carrying the earth in little baskets which they deftly hoisted on their heads. The baskets were filled from the heaps of rubbish in which the precious relics had been buried for long ages, and carried to the deep excavation made for its reception. The long, irregular scurrying groups, interlacing in coming and going, suggested ants at work. They made quite a clamour as they ran, half shouting, half singing.

" I fear we drew M. le Grain from very important work on which his heart was set, and that he could ill spare the time. We felt his polite kindness all the more gracious, knowing this. Afterwards I sat on the Hotel terrace— a good outlook for sunset effects—and watched the exit of the day : the last blaze seemed to set the Nile on fire. I waited for the after-glow, which is even finer than the setting, when the sky, after putting on a sort of mourning, relightens in the west, and the glory grows till the river of water is changed from shore to shore to a river of glowing gold. After this climax, there is a kind of debasement —the gold transmutes to copper—the light begins to fade, till in the west there is left only a broad streak of red, and overhead the blue has turned to deepest violet, almost to black. In this dark setting the stars begin to appear, studding the dark space with the finest points of sparkling light, except for one supreme star that hangs like a lamp in the lofty darkness. This drew the eye to where, not far below, there swam the most exquisitely frail crescent bark that eyes ever beheld. The fineness of it is beyond description. It was a thing of beauty that will live as long as anything lives in my memory."

" I have told of the quiet seas we have had, but even though I repeat, I must speak of the sea to-day at sunset as quite exceptional. There was this evening just the slightest possible heave of the water as of some heavy liquid. The sluggish softness of the slow undulations suggested a sea of liquid metal, and the myriad clear reflections from a uniform pattern of mirror wavelets, made by an almost imperceptible tremor, were in keeping with that idea. As the sun sank towards the horizon, the sky was lit with a splendour of colour I have never seen excelled, and the indefinitely multiplied reflections of this rich band of glowing sky, each one transformed to a long oval, were being simultaneously caught and thrown off by the pulsation of the water, melting, one into the other, and producing a lively kaleidoscopic movement, indescribably beautiful.

" If the enormous field from which the distorted reflections of the lurid sky came is imagined and, in addition, that each element of the complicated pattern is flashing to the eye a metamorphized image of the coloured band of sky as a long oval ring of mixed red and yellow light, the red of the sky band fringing the *inner* edge of each of the million times repeated rings and the yellow their *outer* edge, the blended colours partaking somewhat of the brown and gold of the eye of a peacock's feather, and if, beyond this, it be borne in mind that each oval ring of glittering light is incessantly dilating and contracting, it will be realized that the effect was produced as of a sea covered with myriads of wreathing golden serpents —a living glory, that after the sun's disc vanished, slowly died down. I shall never see another sunset like it.

" It is late evening; night now holds sway. The sky is full of the shimmer of stars. Venus is casting a long lane of light on the blackness of the sea, like that of the moon in our dimmer atmosphere. Orion in his shining armour is high up among the hosts of heaven. The Charioteer is of unwonted brightness, and the Milky Way is a broad pathway of misty light, star strewn. It is already evident from the change of temperature since the sunset that we are rapidly passing from summer warmth to winter cold. We have finished a delightful tour, a real ' grand tour.' "

CHAPTER XII

THE heart trouble of which Sir Joseph Swan had had premonitions ever since 1901 gradually developed, and the necessity for a quieter life and reduced activities became more and more apparent. Medical opinion advised a removal from London.

And so, in the autumn of 1908, a move was made out of London into the quiet of the country. A house (Overhill) had been found at Warlingham, a village on the North Downs of Surrey, in country then scarcely touched by the ever-extending suburbs, and within easy reach of town. It stood on a chalk ridge commanding a wide view of the wold and overlooking, in the valley below, the wooded slopes of Marden Park. John Evelyn had given his advice in the planting of those trees, when he stayed there with his kinsman, Sir Robert Clayton, " a prodigious rich scrivener " of those days. It was Evelyn too who had commented on the profuse growth of the wild thyme and marjoram which still flourish on these chalky hillsides.

The fine air of this country retreat and the undisturbed quiet of his surroundings soon produced a beneficial change in Sir Joseph Swan's health, so that he felt able to take up his experimental work again.

Some outbuildings were easily transformed into laboratory and workshop, and there he resumed his interrupted search for suitable materials for the construction of a voltaic gas battery with imperishable electrolyte, capable of generating electricity in the manner indicated in an earlier chapter.[1] Physical exertion, however, quickly tired him and was apt to cause him pain in the region of the heart; so it was only the lightest manipulative work that he was able to undertake. For the rest, he had to rely upon his assistant and content himself with direct-

[1] See Chapter IX.

ing and superintending the operations. Throughout the greater part of these researches he was assisted by Mr. Eugène Greig, a keen young chemist who proved himself a painstaking and resourceful experimenter. He had also the occasional help of Mr. Dyson, a retired chemical engineer living in the neighbourhood. Dr. Hibbert, a lecturer and demonstrator at the Regent Street Polytechnic, also helped for a while in particular investigations connected with this work.

But although these researches were continued with unabated hopefulness and patience to within a few weeks of his death, he failed to reach the goal he had in view, the construction of a practical form of gas cell. A large amount of information was gained as to the properties and reactions of the materials tried, and many interesting and novel phenomena were observed and recorded, but the results were, on the whole, negative and the problem remained unsolved.

During the summer of 1909 he felt sufficiently well to pay occasional visits to London, and even to undertake a journey to Newcastle to attend to pressing business ; but, as winter approached, the increasing cold again lowered the general level of his strength. However, in February 1910 he writes more hopefully:

" I am going on from strength to strength. In spite of the great storm of wind last night, I slept like a top. I think even stiller than that. Do you know, speaking of tops, that the earth, viewed as a top, is not spinning as steadily as we have been thinking? It has been found that the peg wobbles 15 feet or so radius a year! Everything, it seems, is in a whirl! What wonder if the human atoms that strive so hard to cling to it with such terrible tenacity should now and then get a little dizzy."

During these years at Warlingham there is little to chronicle. Cut off from most of his former activities, and released from the anxieties of business and the hurly-burly of social engagements, he settled down into a quiet uneventful routine. He was able to take things more easily and to rest more. Yet, restful as this time was, work was still the dominating motive of his life. He could not endure to " rust unburnished." For he, too, like the restless Ulysses (in that poem of Tennyson which he loved to quote) had a

> " . . . spirit yearning in desire
> To follow knowledge . . ."

and a heart

> " Made weak by time and fate, but strong in will
> To strive, to seek, to find, and not to yield."

Besides working for an hour or two in the laboratory during the mornings, he would spend much of the rest of the day in reading the technical journals, and in making notes on the scientific work in progress, or drawing neatly-pencilled diagrams of proposed apparatus. When he could be persuaded to divert his mind from these occupations, he greatly enjoyed reading, or having read to him, some novel of the lighter type of romantic fiction ; for example, the exciting narratives of Stanley Weyman, or the whimsical, humorous tales of George Birmingham. Of the former author's books *A Gentleman of France* was his favourite, and the number of copies of this novel which he presented to his friends must at one time have appreciably increased the sales.

Warlingham was beyond the range of easy calling for those living in London, but small parties were occasionally given, and the old scientific friends foregathered. Those who came found him still as eager as ever to hear and discuss the latest achievements and projects of science. To know the latest not only in the world of science, but in the world at large, to keep abreast of the march of events, still remained, as it had always been, his ardent aim. Indeed, now that his retirement cut him off so much from intercourse with the outer world, his appetite for news of all that was going on grew even keener.

In fine weather, when he was feeling well enough to

SIR JOSEPH AND LADY SWAN IN THEIR HOME AT WARLINGHAM

take outdoor exercise, his chief delight was to pace the level path, skirting a field of cultivated lavender, his daughter's hobby, that bounded the southern slope of the garden. Here he was able to tell, for he had stepped it out from end to end, the exact distance he had walked ; here, too, he could gaze to his heart's content upon the wide and varied landscape.

When disinclined for walking, he would take the air, sitting in a revolving summer-house which he called his " sun-trap " and which could be swung with ease to face any quarter. This was a favourite resort of his, and latterly he spent many hours there, being read to, or dictating, or sitting quietly enjoying the view and observing nature, a little wistful that he could no longer hear the high song of the skylark.

Driving had always been a great pleasure to him, and towards the end of 1912 his range of country, hitherto limited by the capacity of a mere horse, was extended by the use of horse-power in the more modern form. He much appreciated the increased comfort and convenience of a car, and the wider explorations into the surrounding country which it made possible.

During 1911 he began to write some autobiographical notes of the early years of his life. These notes, most of which have been incorporated in the present work, though fairly copious in recollections of his boyhood, are few and fragmentary in regard to events of his later life. Whilst he was fluent and at ease in letter-writing, his fastidiousness in other forms of literary composition made the task a tedious one, and he found writing about himself peculiarly difficult and distasteful. Referring to a short account of his invention of the incandescent electric lamp which he had been asked to write by an American journalist, he says : " It is no easy task to say what I ought to say—to pay full measure of acknowledgment to other inventors and yet do justice to myself."

In May 1911 he attended a soirée of the Royal Society and received a hearty greeting from many old friends.

But the effort was as much as his strength could stand. " I durst not stay in the crowd," he writes, " but beat a retreat and remained on the fringe of the throng." This was the last occasion on which he was able to go to the Royal Society or any other public function. Still his scientific work went on, as far as his strength allowed, and the rest of his time was pleasantly and uneventfully spent till, in midsummer 1911, a heavy blow fell upon the family; his youngest daughter, Dorothy, fell ill with pneumonia and died after a brief illness. Her loss was deeply felt. For many years, since the sorrows of 1868, but for the natural passing of the older generation, death had not visited the household; and the swift remove of a loving and much-loved daughter was a terrible shock. Closely following upon this calamity came the serious illness of another daughter. Throughout this period of sorrow and anxiety his letters show with what fortitude he faced these troubles, and with what a resolute but tender spirit of cheerfulness he strove to counteract the besetting depression.

Except for a summer visit to Sidmouth in Devonshire, he spent the year of 1912 quietly at " Overhill," following out his normal routine. On the eve of his birthday he writes :

October 30th, 1912.

" I am full 84 to-day. I feel very thankful that I possess so considerable a measure of healthy life and energy. I have done some work in the laboratory this morning. To-morrow, I intend to take ' a day off.' "

He writes next day (his birthday) in the same strain of thankfulness for " all the good and perfect gifts so lavishly showered upon me during my long life with so much brightness and happiness in it."

It may be observed, in passing, that the large measure of " healthy life " of which he speaks was the heritage of the Swan family as a whole. All his brothers and sisters lived to exceed by many years the allotted span of three score

years and ten. Endowed by nature with a sound constitution and virile physique, he had led a life which, apart
from the strain and stress of work, was well calculated
to preserve his health. Though not a rigid teetotaller,
he seldom took wine, and still more seldom spirits.
He was also, except for a very occasional cigarette for
sociability's sake, a non-smoker. In later life, when
symptoms of heart trouble arose, he began, without becoming a valetudinarian, to study with careful attention
the conditions which gave rise to this trouble so as
to be the better able to guard against it. In this he
was greatly assisted by Dr. Etches, who attended him at
Warlingham, and by the untiring ministrations of Miss
Gosling, a trained nurse, who since 1907 had been living
with the family.

In June 1913 he went to London to attend the wedding
of his son Percival ; and in August a visit was paid to
Thurlestone. His health was well maintained, and his
85th birthday was happily celebrated with a gathering of
many relations and friends.

Harold Begbie, who visited him early in 1914, has given,
with vivid and truthful touch, his impression of Sir Joseph
Swan's personality and his outlook on life. After alluding to the progress of scientific thought and research
during the Victorian era, he says [1]:

" Something of the dignity of this great movement has
communicated itself to his presence. His portraits in
middle life show the stress, almost the harshness of the
movement ; in old age there is nothing but the achievement. It is the grave, dignified face of one who has exer-
cised his soul in great causes, and now, in the hour of
venerable rest, looks backward and looks forward, still
interested, still hopeful, still in love with life. And also
one sees in the thin handsome face, with its flowing beard
and its crest of white hair, the gentleness and the grace of
a soul that has not nailed itself to a single task ; he is an
expert here and there and a great *savant*, but he has loved

[1] *Daily Chronicle*, Jan. 15th, 1914.

poetry and loved nature with the delight of a true amateur. Without anything related to boastfulness or truculence or self-assertion, he tells me quietly and soberly, sitting before a log-fire with a rug over his knees, that he is an optimist, not a pessimist—with a smile and a shake of his head, ' certainly not a pessimist.' He means that life is still good at 85."

Writing again on a later occasion he touches on other aspects of Sir Joseph Swan's philosophy.

" All his life he had cultivated the twin faculties of wonder and reverence, so that in his old age he could look out of the windows of his soul on a world which for him was full of haunting loveliness, on a universe of inviting glory, and on a mystery beyond the power of man to solve, letting the poets take his hand and lead him on where science came to a halt.

" He longed with passion seldom uttered to believe in personality's survival of death, but, hugging this hope to his heart, confessed that the evidence for so sublime a consolation was insufficient for his own conviction. Yet, though he shrank from the thought of annihilation, he was far more troubled, even in his old age, by the military activity of Christian nations. This was the one cloud on the otherwise serene horizon of his declining years. With calm sorrow and mastered indignation he prophesied to me in January 1914 the terrible character of an approaching war, asking, with consternation and perplexity, how Christian Europe could tolerate so visible and so imminent a menace to its culture and its humanity.

" His faith in physical science was profound, but never expressed itself in the truculent manner which is so distressing in youthful materialism. He saw that man must be for ever limited by his senses, and therefore held that, even after science and invention have enormously extended the dominion of mind over matter, humanity will find itself still confronted by the invisible mystery of life itself. Like Pasteur, he bowed himself to the dust at the thought of the Infinite, and, like Shakespeare, saw in the heavens and the earth a mystery which altogether transcends human comprehension.

" Nevertheless, expecting that death might quench his longing for greater knowledge and lasting love, he could not understand ' the tragic outlook.' Surely, he held, the universe in which man finds himself is at every point majestical, and surely science has before her unimaginable triumphs, and surely, too, even if the problem of death remains unsolved to the end of time, humanity has a thousand reasons for gratitude in the beauty of the earth, the friendliness of human relations, and the noble tasks of civilization." [1]

In the spring of 1914 the Corporation of Newcastle passed a resolution offering to confer upon him the freedom of the city. This signal recognition by his fellow-townsmen gave him great pleasure. In accepting the honour, he asked, however, that the ceremony of the presentation might be deferred until later in the year, when it was hoped that the warmer weather would enable him to undertake the journey to Newcastle with less risk. In the meantime his mind went back to recall the strenuous and eventful years he had spent as a Tynesider; and he began to jot down notes for the coming speech. He looked forward, too, with pleasure to meeting his friend Sir Charles Parsons, who was to receive the freedom of the city at the same time.

But his strength was failing. He required to rest more frequently. A tiresome cough which had troubled him intermittently of late grew more persistent and exhausting. In his letters the handwriting, normally so bold and full of energy, was getting shaky and the matter briefer. But the tone was still happy. He was still able to enjoy, as of old, his siesta in his " sun trap " and the visits of friends, and he continued to be keenly interested in all that went on.

So it was till the end of April when, with a sudden change of the weather from summer-like warmth to wintry

[1] *The Times*, Oct. 31st, 1928.

cold, his health too suffered a marked change. He lost to
a great extent his interest and pleasure in things around
him. He seemed also to lose the will to make any exertion. Sir Thomas Barlow, whom he had consulted on
former occasions, was called in on May 26th. He pro-
nounced him to be very ill, but no immediate danger
was anticipated. But on the same night came a sudden
collapse through heart weakness, and in the early hours
of May 27th he passed peacefully away.

He was laid to rest in the churchyard at Warlingham.
Upon one tablet of the carved tomb which marks his
grave are inscribed the lines from Tennyson's *Day
Dream*, which were often on his lips :

> " Were it not a pleasant thing
>   To fall asleep with all one's friends;
> To sleep thro' terms of mighty wars,
>   And wake on science grown to more,
> On secrets of the brain, the stars,
>   As wild as aught of fairy lore."

And so, two months before the outbreak of the mightiest
war the world has seen, he fell asleep.

The ceremony of the presentation of the freedom of the
city of Newcastle, thus sadly frustrated, was not, however,
abandoned, but took place some two months after his
death, his son Kenneth being deputed by the family to
act as his representative and to accept from the Lord
Mayor, Sir Johnstone Wallace, the gift of Tyne plate
which Sir Joseph Swan had chosen, in preference to the
more usual casket, to commemorate his enrolment as a
freeman.

From the foregoing chapters the reader will have
gathered some idea of those qualities of mind and temperament which contributed to Sir Joseph Swan's success
as an inventor. At all periods of his life his mind
was extraordinarily alert and observant. He was quick
to seize upon new facts and new conceptions ; prompt
to acquire and master all kinds of new knowledge and to

familiarize himself with the properties and reactions of all manner of materials. To this faculty of acute observation and rapid assimilation was coupled an unusually retentive memory. Hence came that almost inexhaustible fertility of expedient and resource which characterized all his experimental work. Add also an untiring patience and persistence in following up the train of his ideas, and, in working them out, an infinite capacity for taking pains. But behind all this was the motive power which brings the inventive faculty into play: that inscrutable psychological complex, made up of imagination, prophetic vision and, above all, the instinctive desire, which with him was an irresistible impulse, to improve and perfect the existing means of doing things.

In these pages Sir Joseph Swan has been portrayed mainly as an inventor ; so perhaps he would wish to be described and remembered; but in truth that is only a limited aspect of his character. He was more than an inventor; he was, in the fullest and truest sense, a philosopher, a lover of knowledge; not merely that knowledge which falls within the domain of science, but knowledge in its widest scope ; knowledge which includes the whole range of natural phenomena. To know and understand more about the nature of things, to win some fresh secret from Nature's exhaustless store of marvels and mysteries, that was the ever-impelling passion of his life. Closely akin to this instinctive longing, and equally strong, was his love of beauty in Nature. For him all the wonders of Science were as nothing matched with the grandeur of a thunderstorm or the " heavenly alchemy " of a sunset or a summer's day.

Something has been said of his modest and unassuming manner. This was only one of the many captivating traits of his character. His habitual temper was one of considerate gentleness, graced by a chivalrous courtesy, which with him was second nature. In every way he was the soul of generosity. Those who sought his advice never asked in vain ; and those who came to consult him never failed to receive the best that he could give. No wonder that his friends were many, and that, under the genial influence of his personality, acquaintance quickly ripened into friendship and friendship into affection.

Yet ever beneath his gentleness and courtesy there flowed a tranquil undercurrent of dignity and power. One who knew him well writes that " no picture of him would be complete which did not convey the impression of his quiet, massive strength of purpose and that big simplicity, so compelling that no one ever expected him to be anything but his original self or to diverge one hair's breadth from his own way."

Such is the picture of Sir Joseph Swan that those who knew him will retain. But his claim to be remembered extends beyond the limited range of personal acquaintance, and rests not merely upon those traits of character which endeared him to his friends; it stands upon the broader and more permanent foundation of public service. His work remains and bears fruit, marking him out as an inventor whose achievements have brought about far-reaching developments in industry, and as a benefactor who has added not a little to the comfort and amenity of the conditions under which we live.

INDEX

A

Addresses by J. W. Swan, 130-138 : at opening of the electro-technical laboratories at Liverpool, 138 ; as President of the Institution of Electrical Engineers, 131, 132 ; as President of the Pharmaceutical Society, 134 ; as President of the Society of Chemical Industry, 156

Annan, J. Craig, 125
—— Thomas, 39, 125
Archer, William Scott, 34
Armstrong, Sir William (Lord Armstrong), 65, 71, 75, 86, 90, 128, 155
Artificial cellulose thread, 9, 98-100
—— silk, 9, 99, 100, 101
"Ashfield," 51, 111, 120
Austen, Sir W. Roberts, 153, 154
Autotype process, 9, 39, 137
Ayrton, Mrs. Hertha, 132, 141
—— Professor W. E., 72, 132, 141

B

Baker, Sir Benjamin, 141
Barclay, Sir Thomas, 30
Barlow, Sir Thomas, 174
Barrett, Sir William, 141
Becquerel, M. Edmond, 35
Begbie, Harold, 171-173
Bell, Sir Isaac Lowthian, 154
Benson, Sir Frank, 149
Benwell, factory at, 73, 82, 87
Bewick, Thomas, 45
Blakey & Hurman, Messrs., 49
Boussod, Messrs., Valledon et Cie., 40
Brady, Captain, R.E., 150
—— Henry, 136
Bramwell, Sir Frederick, 86, 123

Braun, Messrs., 39
British Association meetings : in 1882, at Southampton, 90-93 ; in 1886, at Birmingham, 113-115
Bromide printing paper, 9, 44
Bromley and neighbourhood, 94-98, 105
Brush Company, 83
Burt, Thomas, M.P., 113

C

Cameron, George, 12, 13
—— Mrs. George, 28
—— Isabella (see also Swan), 11, 12
—— Robert, 17
Cameron-Swan, Donald, 125-127
Carbon process, 9, 30, 31, 37-39, 41, 137
Carland, 22
Carte, D'Oyley, 78
Carter, Sydney, 49
Cellular lead plate storage battery (see Storage battery)
Chamberlain, Richard, 113
Chardonnet, Count Hilaire de, 100
Chemical Society, Newcastle-on-Tyne, 64
Chrome tanning, 41, 42
City of Richmond, Inman Line, 75
Clark, Latimer, 72, 131, 132
Clayton, Sir Robert, 166
Collings, Jesse, M.P., 47, 113
Collodion, 29, 33-35, 43, 48
Communist leaders, trial of (Rossel, Ferré and Bourgeois), 52
Connett, Professor, 112
Courtaulds, Messrs., 100
Courtney, Leonard (Lord Courtney), 148
Cowen, Joseph, M.P., 148, 149
—— Sir Joseph, 29
Coxon, James, 75

M   177

APPENDIX

LECTURE GIVEN BY DR. JOHN ALDINGTON IN 1959

I FEEL privileged to have been asked by the Illuminating Engineering Society to speak on this historic occasion in the very room, and at the very time eighty years later, where Sir Joseph Swan made his first public announcement of the development of the incandescent electric lamp. There had been limited announcements before, but this was his first public announcement of the successful—and the important word is successful—development of the carbon filament lamp. I feel, too, something of the atmosphere of this room in which your Literary and Philosophical Society has met for so many years ; an occasion which I feel sure inspired the young Swan as he listened here to other lectures long before his announcement in 1879. I am conscious this evening of the same sense of occasion that must have impressed the audience when Sir William Armstrong took the chair and Joseph Swan gave his momentous news to the citizens of your great city.

I propose, Mr. Chairman, to separate our considerations into three parts.

Firstly I propose to tell you something of the life and work of Joseph Swan, omitting the work that led up to the production of a practical incandescent lamp. Secondly I shall give some account of the thirty years of persistent effort that he devoted to the seemingly insuperable problem of making a successful incandescent lamp. Finally I should like to speak from my own personal experience of the past thirty-five years, in which we have seen how much has been built on the foundations of modern electric lighting so successfully laid by Joseph Wilson Swan.

Born in Sunderland in 1828, Joseph Swan wrote in his old age these words : " The days of my youth extend backwards to the dark ages, for I was born when the rushlight, the tallow dip and the solitary blaze of the hearth were common means of indoor lighting. An infrequent glass bowl on a wooden post containing a cupful of evil-smelling train-oil with a crude cotton wick stuck in it so as to make darkness visible out of doors. In the chambers of the great the wax candle relieved the gloom on state occasions, but as a rule the common people went to bed soon after sunset."

Joseph Swan spent his early childhood in this industrial area and I believe that this fact had a great deal to do with the contributions which he was later to make to many different fields of human endeavour. He says : " I roamed about with my brother John and we did not close our eyes except in sleep. I knew the tailor's and the cobbler's art so far as these can be known by early and careful observation. I knew, too, how nails and candles were made." Lime kilns, and factories for making crucibles, glass bottle making, brick making, rope making, the gas works—these were the things that Joseph Swan saw and studied and which made such impression on his mind in his early youth.

He was first sent to a dame-school " kept by three dear old ladies "—and from there he went to a large boys' school near Sunderland until he was thirteen. Later he wrote this : " I feel strongly that acquaintance with these newly discovered arts, from the time of their birth, greatly added to their impressiveness, giving them a vivid interest which those who have only been acquainted with them after they have attained a certain maturity and become common knowledge, altogether miss. The elation created by the announcement of a great discovery, and first acquaintance with its results, is a sensation of an extraordinarily uplifting character and I can never forget its effect as a stimulus to experimental effort." In those words we have epitomised something of the life and character of Joseph Swan, a man very conscious indeed of the fact that invention and development is a progressive thing. A man who realised that none of us, neither then nor in these latter days, is able to make a unique development or invention in vacuo, but that we depend on all the past as we look into the future. There was no man more ready than Joseph Swan to acknowledge the contributions of the early pioneers upon whose work he built.

In 1841 his interest in electricity was roused, while he was still at school, by a friend of the family who possessed a Wimshurst machine and a few Leyden jars.

He was apprenticed for six years to a Sunderland firm of druggists but, both principals having died after three years, his apprenticeship was broken and he subsequently joined his friend John Mawson in his business as chemist and druggist at Newcastle. During those three years—it should be remembered that we are still talking of a boy of fourteen to seventeen —he became a member of the Sunderland Athenaeum and so gained access to a good library. He was now able to add to his own observations of the things around him, readings from the works of great men of the past. He attributed his early interest in electric lighting to his readings of J. W. Star's *Electric Lamp*. Star was an American who died at the untimely age of twenty-five and there is no doubt that had Star lived he would have made other major contributions to the eventual solution of the problem of the electric lamp. But it was not to be. Star died, as I have said, as a young man. In his short lifetime, however, he showed how a filament could be made to glow by the passage of electric current when the filament was enclosed in the vacuum at the top of a barometer tube. Young Swan knew about that in 1845. He listened to lectures in this very lecture theatre, by Staite. Staite's lectures showed the carbon arc and also a platinum wire heated to incandescence by the passage of current.

In 1846 young Swan joined Mawson, and before long began the manufacture of collodion for which the firm of Mawson and Swan became famous. Indeed his formula for photographic collodion, established in 1856, remained unaltered for ninety years.

In 1856 and onwards, Swan became interested in the production of permanent photographic prints free from the defects of fading. He was aware of work done some twenty or thirty years before in which it had been shown that certain materials containing gelatine and potassium chromate were rendered relatively insoluble by exposure to light. But all attempts to produce high definition pictures by such means, although interesting, failed to reproduce the fine detail without which the process was of no permanent value.

Swan, knowing of that work and pondering over it, made the remarkable observation, and reached the correct conclusion, that the solution of the gelatine film was taking place from the wrong side. What was needed was to dissolve away the film from the side opposite to that on which it had been exposed to light.

He showed also how it was possible to transfer the film, by the so-called carbon process, and thus produce photographs of high definition and complete permanence. Sir Kenneth tells me that he has in his possession photographs made by this process which are as good today as they were ninety or a hundred years ago when they were first produced.

The achievements of Swan in this field opened up a great area of work in photographic reproduction. The process was patented and the patents were sold to what has become the Autotype Company. We have in the possession of my own company an oil painting of Sir Joseph Wilson Swan. We photographed that painting and, after we had acquainted them of this occasion tonight the Autotype Company produced by the original process a high definition reproduction of it. I hope to be able to hand to Sir Kenneth, and to the Lord Mayor of Newcastle and to their worships the Mayor of Sunderland and the Mayor of Gateshead, copies of this reproduction.

Arising from that work, Swan saw that it would be possible to use modifications of his invention to produce high definition copper-plates capable of being used for high-speed printing. Here again the method was taken over by the Autotype Company and they have, without my knowing it, prepared specially, by the carbon process, a print from the copper which controls the etching of photogravure printing cylinders or plates. The proper place for this to rest is in the hands of Sir Kenneth Swan and I shall be glad if he will accept it.

You will appreciate that the work I have just described, and the proper understanding of the processes which take place in the hardening of gelatine by the action of light in the presence of a chromate, had other possibilities. Joseph Swan recognised that the methods of tanning leather might be improved by substituting chromium salts for the iron salts then used, and he was the first to suggest the chromating of leather to transform it from ordinary hide into the finished product.

In 1871 Dr. R. L. Maddock proposed the use of gelatine in place of collodion as a vehicle for the silver bromide on photographic plates, thus introducing the dry process of photography : but the resulting dry plates were slow and lacking in density. Swan critically examined the defects of the dry plates and found that by careful temperature control of the process of manufacture he could so improve its sensitiveness and reliability that the art of photography was revolutionised. His interest in photography then being most strongly engaged he went further, and, although it may not be known to you in this hall, he was the inventor of bromide printing paper which is still used today for enlarging.

In 1879 Swan exhibited an improvement of Plante's lead-acid accumulator. The Plante lead-acid accumulator was originally made by immersing two sheets of lead in sulphuric acid and by alternately charging and discharging the cell so formed. In October 1879 Swan exhibited an improvement on this device. It consisted of attaching frills of lead foil to the plates to increase the ratio of surface area to total size and weight. Later he took the further step of depositing spongy lead on the plates, and between the frills, by electrolytic action; and, later still, he designed a cellular plate, similar to the ones used today, into the cavities of which the spongy lead could be compressed. This was patented in 1881. In the grounds of the lamp works at Ponders End, which was the site of the Edison and Swan companies' first works, we still make lead-acid accumulators today.

1879–80 also saw the climax in Swan's search for a satisfactory incandescent lamp, but I propose to deal with that separately.

In 1883 Swan's search for an homogeneous non-fibrous material for lamp filaments led to the discovery of artificial silk. He nitrated his paper or his cotton threads, dissolved the resulting mass of cellulose in acetic acid, and forced it through a die into a coagulating fluid. The resulting filament was tenuous, lustrous and continuous, and could be drawn down to an extremely fine thread. This suggested to Swan its use as a textile and Mrs. Swan was persuaded to crochet some of it into mats and doyleys which were exhibited at the Inventors Exhibition in 1885. Some, I believe, are in the Museum here and some in the Science Museum in London. He patented the process in 1883 and I propose to try to show you exactly what he did.

(The lecturer then gave a demonstration of the extrusion of nitro-cellulose into a coagulant, and produced a length of fine fibre.)

Early in 1883, with the formation of the joint company with Edison and with the establishment of the factory at Ponders End, the Swan family moved to a new house, " Lauriston ", Bromley, Kent. The home was lighted by incandescent lamps throughout, and these were fed from a small generating plant and storage battery on the premises. The lamps were Swan's, the storage battery was Swan's, the generator was made by Swan in his own workshop. The gas engine driving the dynamo was Swan's own design and, except for the castings, was constructed in his own workshop on the premises.

In 1892 he engaged John Rhodin, a young Swedish chemist, as an assistant, and together they undertook an extensive research on the electrolytic deposition of copper.

It had been realised for some time that the conductivity of copper wire was critically dependant on its purity. If, therefore, it could be shown that copper could be manufactured in a highly purified form by electrolysis, large savings in capital outlay on the cables connecting Siemen's dynamos with Swan's lamps were possible.

In 1894 the results of this work were communicated to the Royal Society and Swan's election to a Fellowship resulted. In the same year he moved from Bromley to Holland Park —again with a laboratory and workshop in the basement—because of his increasingly numerous scientific and business engagements in London itself.

He was elected to the Council of the Royal Society, made a visitor of the Royal Institution, and the Board of the National Physical Laboratory. In 1898 he became President of the Institute of Electrical Engineers ; in 1900 President of the Society of Chemical Industry. In 1901 the University of Durham conferred upon him the degree of Doctor of Science ; he was already a Master of Arts. In 1902 he was awarded the Progress Medal of the Royal Photographic Society for his invention of the carbon process. In 1904 he was awarded the Hughes' Medal of the Royal Society and a knighthood was conferred upon him in November of that year. In 1906 the Prince of Wales, President of the Society of Arts, presented him with the Albert Medal. These are remarkable achievements for a man who left school at the age of thirteen and received no formal scientific education.

In 1908 he retired to " Overhill ", Warlingham, Surrey, when eighty years old, and established a laboratory and workshop in outbuildings. In 1914 at a special assembly the Corporation of Newcastle offered him the freedom of the city, but his failing health precluded so long a journey. He died on 27th May 1914.

I want to read, in concluding this first factual section, from an appreciation of one aspect of his life by Harold Begbie, who visited him early in 1914. Begbie says, among other things, " All his life he had cultivated the twin faculties of wonder and reverence so that, in his old age, he could look out of the window of his soul on a world which for him was full of haunting loveliness, on a universe of inviting glory, and on a mystery beyond the power of man to solve, letting the poets take his hand and lead him on where science came to a halt."

With those words, Mr. Chairman, my Lord Mayor and your Worships, I conclude this first part of the account of Swan's life.

Second Part

The discovery of the voltaic cell and the heating effect of an electric current flowing in a wire suggested to many inventors that an incandescent wire might be used as a small and convenient unit of light for domestic purposes. Almost the only metals with sufficiently high melting points available in the first half of the nineteenth century were platinum and iridium, and alloys of these two metals. They were also the only metals that could be used because they alone had the property of a very low rate of oxidation when heated in air.

As I said, the early workers—there were many—thought that the filament of the lamp would last longer if the air could be excluded. They thought that to do this the filament should in some way be mounted inside an envelope exhausted of air. But we have to appreciate that there were no high vacuum-pumps ; merely manually operated pumps which would give a degree of vacuum which we now know to be quite inadequate to ensure the non-oxidation condition recognised as necessary by these early workers.

Swan had read of the work of Star and had listened to the lectures of Staite in 1848. Between the years 1848–55 he had conceived the idea that carbon, if it could be made sufficiently strong and flexible, would be far better than any metal as a filament, because it clearly had a higher melting point. He produced in those years some " beautifully thin and flexible twists and spirals of carbonised paper ". (I am quoting from Joseph Swan's own record.) He also observed that the products of the carbonisation of parchmentised paper were exceptionally solid in texture and highly elastic and strong. That observation, in my opinion, is the key to the decisive superiority of the Swan lamps of 1881 and onwards over the carbonised bamboo filaments of Edison. In 1860 Swan himself mounted some of these paper loops and spirals which he had carbonised by heating in charcoal in a crucible. He mounted them in the form of an arch on the electrodes inside a bell jar exhausted by a manual air pump. Of course, there were no sources of electrical supply as we know them today. He used primary cells—fifty cells connected in series—and he found that the carbonised paper could be heated to incandescence, but the paper disintegrated in a few minutes and blackened the containing vessel. Swan correctly recognised that this was due to the fact that he was unable to produce the necessary degree of vacuum, and he registered this observation in his mind. One must realise, of course, that he was carrying on his business with Mawson as a chemist and druggist in Newcastle ; these other things were his hobby. He recognised that carbon was not necessarily the wrong material. It was certainly the only material available, apart from platinum and iridium, that would not melt at incandescent temperature.

Swan was encouraged, in 1875, to restart his work on the lamp by the publication of Crookes' research on electrical discharges through rarefied gases. Crookes' work was made possible by Sprengel's invention, in 1865, of the mercury pump. This gave a far better vacuum than the mechanical pumps that preceded it.

He induced Stearn, who was then working in Birkenhead, and had experience both of the Sprengel pump and of glass-blowing, to assist him at this stage.

Swan had held the conviction for many years that, given the correct operating conditions, carbon was probably a satisfactory material for lamp filaments. He intended, initially, to avoid the difficulties of manipulating thin paper or thread filaments, and he used a carbon rod about 1 mm. in diameter for the first batch of lamps to be made under the new conditions. Not only did he have the bulbs evacuated to a much higher degree than ever before, but he introduced the process of heating the glass bulbs while pumping them, to drive off the occluded gas on their inner surfaces. The necessity for this process was in itself a very important discovery at that time, much as we should take it for granted at the present day.

It must have been a great disappointment to Swan when he found that despite the higher vacuum and the heating of the bulbs, the finished lamps still quickly blackened when lit. It occurred to him that this might be due to gas emitted by the carbon filament itself, after " sealing off ".

He then conceived the idea of passing current through the filament during the last stage of the exhaust process, while the lamp was still on the pump. At this stage, when little gas is left to be trapped between the falling globules of mercury, the pump commences to "click", and successive globules fall freely and rather noisily on to the ones ahead. One can imagine the tremendous surge of hope with which he must have been filled when, as the filament heated up the clicking noise ceased, thus showing that a further emission of gas was being swept away. He must have waited with renewed enthusiasm for the time when the last trace of gas was removed, when the pump again emitted the characteristic clicks, and he could hope that he had at last produced the first workable carbon filament lamp ever to be known to the world.

I now want to make some reference to the work of Edison. On the one hand we have Swan, working almost alone, experimenting with lamps as a hobby while carrying on his daily work as a chemist and druggist. In America there was Thomas Alva Edison, a man of magnificent achievement, a man to whom the world owes so much. He had invented systems of duplex and quadruplex telegraphy, and was working on a carbon microphone and a unique loud-speaking receiver, amongst many other devices. His work was directed to the many and various ways in which electricity could be employed in the service of man.

Ideas associated with the " division of the electric light " occurred almost simultaneously to Edison and to Swan : but whereas the latter was labouring almost single-handed, the former had some eighty or ninety assistants in his laboratory at Menlo Park. He tackled the problem of the incandescent lamp while working on many other things. His background was electrical communications rather than chemistry.

Let me however make this clear : Swan himself has recorded that he was—" led to ponder the question "—of incandescent lighting before Edison was born. The problem was almost continuously in his mind until the year of ultimate success—1878–79.

Although each knew of the other's work the two never met, but that did not influence the final result. There was, moreover, a fundamental difference of approach between the two. Edison was an opportunist of a very high order : and all credit to him. Immediately he saw the remote possibility of producing a commercial electric lamp he patented and published his work. He patented it in America ; he patented it in England ; he patented every advance he made. He took out a broad patent in 1879 covering the principle of mounting an incandescent carbon or other filament inside a glass bulb exhausted of air. Now there are those of us, and I am included in this number, who consider that, due to Star's work and earlier publications, this was not patentable matter. That was also the belief of Joseph Swan and for this reason he did not himself take out a patent.

I believe that the existence of the Edison Patents, weak though they may have been, is the main reason why there has been a tendency, during the past eighty years, to ascribe to him, and not to Swan, the original work that made the first carbon filament lamp possible. My own investigations of the facts, consideration of the dates involved, and of the unique contributions which were made by both men, cause me to state most categorically that it was Swan who made the fundamental invention which resulted in a practicable carbon filament lamp, the precursor of the lamps of the future. And it was Swan who after these two men had joined forces—and I am glad that they did come together instead of fighting each other in harmful litigation—it was Swan who took the further step that produced from these early beginnings the actual practical lamps in 1882 and 1883 and onwards, which were manufactured in such large quantities so quickly. More than ten thousand lamps were produced each week in the first factory in 1883.

Edison experimented with some 1600 different earths, minerals and ores in his search for the ideal filament material. He turned his attention from metals to cotton thread, but he did not discover Swan's parchmentising technique and eventually abandoned cotton for bamboo fibre. He examined no fewer than 6000 species of bamboo-like plants, obtained from all over the world.

Swan, on the other hand, did not consider that natural fibre, such as untreated cotton thread or bamboo, possessed the physical characteristics for which he was searching. He discovered, however, that when cotton fibre is immersed in sulphuric acid it becomes parchmentised, or " mercerised ". The natural fibre agglutinates, shrinks and has the appearance of catgut : and the lamps made by him between 1880 and 1883 incorporated this material.

In 1883, Swan proceeded to the further development of dissolving nitro-cellulose in acetic acid, forcing the product through a jet to produce a continuous fibre the diameter of which was related to the diameter of the jet. This fibre was subsequently denitrified, and carbonised by heating it in charcoal. Thus were produced the beautiful filaments of electric lamps which survived for more than thirty years as the luminous body inside the exhausted glass bulb. They survive today in certain special lamps such as telephone lamps, and they are still manufactured by the identical process.

I want now to leave the work of Swan but, in leaving it, I want to read you a definition of Swan's own on the subject of inventors and inventions. I think that you will appreciate from this the reason which prevented Swan patenting all the experimental steps he took. I submit that Swan was wrong, but high honour is due to him for the way in which he looked at these things. It may have prevented him receiving the full honours—he received many honours, but perhaps not the full honours—that were due to him.

" An inventor is an opportunist who takes occasion by the hand and, having seen where some want exists, successfully applies the right means to attain the desired end ; the means may be largely or even wholly something already known, or there may be certain originality or discovery in the means employed, but in every case the inventor " remembers that "—in every case the inventor uses the work of others. If I may use a metaphor, I should liken him to the man who essays the conquest of some virgin alp. At the outset he scans the beaten track and as he progresses in the ascent he uses the steps used by those who have preceded him wherever they lead in the right direction, and it is only after the last footprints have died out, that he takes the ice axe in his hands and cuts the remaining steps, few or many, that lift him to the crowning height which is his goal."

Third Part

Now, Mr. Chairman, I propose to give you some account of the present state of the art in the field of light source development.

Carbon was eventually superseded by the successful development of the tungsten filament. Tungsten is the most refractory of all the elements. For a long time methods of producing ductile tungsten wire eluded the investigator but eventually Coolidge in America showed how, by producing crystals of tungsten of the right mixture of grain size, the tungsten powder could be compressed into a bar and then sintered into rods at a temperature below the melting point. This sintered material with its crude rough crystalline structure and many interstices was then found to be malleable at temperatures of the order of 1500 degrees C., and in suitable conditions could be swaged at those temperatures into rods and eventually drawn into wire.

Tungsten filaments produced in that way are the filaments of the electric lamps of today.

Tungsten is a unique material, and has the highest melting point of all the metallic elements. It is, therefore, unlikely, in my opinion, that it will ever be superseded as the refractory filament of the incandescent electric lamp. It enables lamps to be made of 10 kW. and even 50 kW. on the one hand, and of a fraction of a watt on the other. In the small sizes the lamps can be inserted into surgical instruments capable themselves of being inserted into the cavities of the human body.

Apart altogether from the range of lamps which are known to us in our households and in lighting this room tonight there are more than 10,000 different designs of tungsten filament lamps in current production in the lamp factories of the world. The efficiency has been progressively increased by a study of the metallurgy of tungsten : by reducing the thermal losses from the filaments, by arranging the filament first in a single coil—and there is about a yard of wire in such a filament—then into a coiled coil, and in special cases, into a triple coil.

Various gases have been used to fill the previously evacuated bulb ; nitrogen, argon, and various mixtures of these two ; also krypton, and even xenon have been employed. The purpose, of course, is to enable the filament to be run at temperatures as close as possible to the melting point of tungsten without excessive volatilisation.

The first Swan lamp operated at 1·7 lumens per watt. Special lamps made during the war operated with their filaments very near the melting point of tungsten, and these gave as much as 45 lumens per watt. The more normal figure that we have to think of is 10 lumens per watt for a small household bulb, and 25 to 30 lumens per watt for a projector lamp. A tungsten filament is capable of being operated through the whole range of temperatures corresponding to these different efficiencies.

As the filament temperature is increased the radiation moves through the infra-red region to the visible region of the spectrum, until, at the melting point of tungsten, an efficiency of more than 50 lumens per watt is achieved.

The practical problem is to strike a balance between the efficiency and the life of the lamp. A tungsten lamp may be given a life of 5 minutes or of 5 thousand hours. But the efficiency will be widely different in the two cases. The point at which the balance is struck is governed by the use to which the lamp will be put.

I must now pass quickly on to give some account of the electrical discharge lamp. It has long been known that a luminous discharge will take place in a tube that has been partially evacuated and connected to a high voltage supply. The colour of the emitted light is governed by the nature, the temperature and the pressure of the residual gas in the tube.

(A demonstration was then given of a tube containing neon gas and a globule of mercury. When first struck this tube gives the characteristic red colour associated with neon, but as it warms up and the mercury vaporises, the colour changes to the well-known mercury blue light.)

The efficiency of such devices was at first low, because of the power required to heat the electrodes ; but it was discovered later that if the pressure of the mercury was allowed to rise to one atmosphere or more, efficiencies some thirty times that of the original Swan lamp, or three to four times that of a tungsten lamp of similar wattage, could be obtained. From these beginnings came the use of higher and higher pressures with the development of quartz lamps until eventually we were enabled to produce lamps with a centre-arc brightness greater than that of the sun's disk as viewed from the earth. These lamps were used in searchlights during the war, to enable the searchlight teams to be reduced in number, and eventually automatic searchlights to be produced without men on the site.

Attention was frequently turned to studies of the rarer gases. It was thought that the arc spectrum of mercury had certain inherent limitations, and that if we employed gases of great atomic complexity it might be possible to break away from the distorting semi-monochromatic emission of mercury (and of course that of the sodium lamp, with its strong yellow light) and produce a virtual continuum of visible radiation.

During the war, when working in that field with Professor Edgerton of the Massachusetts Institute of Technology, we found it possible to use the extremely rare element xenon, present in the earth's atmosphere to the extent of about one part in 10 million. It was proposed to excite it under conditions of such high current density that a virtual white light continuum was produced, similar to north daylight.

(A demonstration was then given of a xenon arc used for stroboscopic purposes.)

This 500 watt xenon arc has a daylight quality and great stability of output. It is therefore eminently suitable for cinema projection and is being increasingly used for that purpose.

It has a further valuable property for projection use. When run on alternating current, the arc strikes and fades away almost instantaneously. This makes it possible to dispense with the " shutter " that is an essential part of the normal cinema projector, provided that successive " frames " on the film are moved forward in synchronism with the alternations of the arc current.

There is no doubt in my mind that the xenon gas arc is destined to play an increasing part as a light source particularly for projection purposes.

The discharge used for the projection of the film you have just seen produces not only visible light but also ultra-violet radiation. When this radiation impinges on certain chemicals, such as those with which the inside surface of this beaker is coated, it is transformed in frequency from the ultra-violet to the visible region. The wavelength of the resulting light depends on the chemical constitution of the powder. By suitably selecting and mixing the chemicals the ultra-violet radiation can be transformed into light of almost any colour. (A demonstration of fluorescence in several different colours was given at this point.)

I have already mentioned that the efficiency of discharge lamps, in terms of visible light output for a given electrical input, at first compared unfavourably with other light sources because of the electrical power dissipated in the electrodes. In the mid-thirties, however, electrodes coated with alkaline earth compounds were introduced. These electrodes have the property of giving rise to copious electron emission at much lower temperatures than the plain metallic electrodes previously used. The power wasted was therefore materially reduced and fluorescent tubes, as we know them today, became an economic possibility. This development, together with subsequent improvements in the colour rendering of the fluorescent powders, has brought the overall efficiency of modern tubes up to five times that of equivalent tungsten filament lamps, combined with a much longer life.

(A final demonstration was given at this point. It consisted in illuminating with U.V. light a picture of Sir Joseph Swan that had been painted in fluorescent powder. When the U.V. lamps were switched on, the panel, which had previously appeared as a patchwork of dull grey and fawns, glowed in its true colours and revealed itself as an excellent colour portrait. The lecturer asked Sir Kenneth Swan to unveil this portrait as the U.V. light was switched on.)

Lecture given by Dr. John Aldington in Newcastle, in 1959.